D1282988

THE QUIET REBELS

The aim of Zenith Books is to present the history of minority groups in the United States and their participation in the growth and development of the country. Through histories and biographies written by leading historians in collaboration with established writers for young people, Zenith Books will increase the awareness of minority group members of their own heritage and at the same time develop among all people an understanding and appreciation of that heritage.

DR. JOHN HOPE FRANKLIN, Chairman of the History Department at the University of Chicago, has also taught at Brooklyn College, Fisk University, and Howard University. For the year 1962–63, he was William Pitt Professor of American History and Institutions at Cambridge University in England. He is the author of many books, including FROM SLAVERY TO FREEDOM, THE MILITANT SOUTH, RECONSTRUCTION AFTER THE CIVIL WAR, and THE EMANCIPATION PROCLAMATION.

SHELLEY UMANS is Director of the Center for Innovation for the Board of Education of the City of New York, a specialist in reading instruction, and a member of the instructional staff of Teachers College, Columbia University. For more than ten years she has been a consultant to many major urban school systems throughout the United States. She is the author of NEW TRENDS IN READING INSTRUCTION, DESIGNS FOR READING PROGRAMS, and co-author of TEACHING THE DISADVANTAGED.

PHILIP STERLING was formerly associated with CBS Radio, where he was Assistant Director of Press Information. He is the author of LAUGHING ON THE OUTSIDE, and co-author of POLIO PIONEERS, FIORELLO LA GUARDIA, and the Zenith book FOUR TOOK FREEDOM.

DR. MARIA BRAU is assistant professor of history at Howard University in Washington, D.C., and author of another Zenith book, ISLAND IN THE CROSSROADS. Her grandfather, Salvador Brau, was the leading historian of Puerto Rico.

TRACY SUGARMAN graduated from the Syracuse University School of Fine Arts and studied at the Art School of the Brooklyn Museum. Among the books he has illustrated are FEELING OF JAZZ, I HAVE A DREAM, and the Zenith book THE UNFINISHED MARCH. He is also the author of STRANGER AT THE GATES.

Other Outstanding Zenith Books

FOUR TOOK FREEDOM, by Philip Sterling and Rayford Logan. The lives of Harriet Tubman, Frederick Douglass, Robert Smalls, and Blanche K. Bruce.

A GLORIOUS AGE IN AFRICA, by Daniel Chu and Elliott Skinner. The story of three great African empires.

GREAT RULERS OF THE AFRICAN PAST, by Lavinia Dobler and William A. Brown, with special consultant Philip Curtin. Five African rulers who led their nations in times of crisis.

A GUIDE TO AFRICAN HISTORY, by Basil Davidson, revised and edited by Haskel Frankel. A general survey of the African past from earliest times to the present.

ISLAND IN THE CROSSROADS, by M. M. Brau. The history of Puerto Rico.

LIFT EVERY VOICE, by Dorothy Sterling and Benjamin Quarles. The lives of Booker T. Washington, W. E. B. Du Bois, Mary Church Terrell, and James Weldon Johnson.

PASSAGE TO THE GOLDEN GATE, by Daniel Chu and Samuel C. Chu. A history of the Chinese in America to 1910.

PIONEERS AND PATRIOTS, by Lavinia Dobler and Edgar A. Toppin. The lives of six Negroes of the colonial and revolutionary eras.

TIME OF TRIAL, TIME OF HOPE, by Milton Meltzer and August Meier. The history of the Negro in America from 1919 to 1941.

THE UNFINISHED MARCH, by Carol Drisko and Edgar Toppin. The Negro in the United States from Reconstruction to World War I.

WORTH FIGHTING FOR, by Agnes McCarthy and Lawrence Reddick. A history of the Negro in the United States during the Civil War and Reconstruction.

THE QUIET REBELS
Four Puerto Rican Leaders

José Celso Barbosa · Luis Muñoz Rivera
José de Diego · Luis Muñoz Marín

by Philip Sterling and
Maria Brau, ~~Ph.D.~~

Illustrated by
Tracy Sugarman

J920
St
c.2

ZENITH BOOKS
DOUBLEDAY & COMPANY, INC.   GARDEN CITY, NEW YORK
1968

The Zenith Books edition, published simultaneously in hardbound and paperback volumes, is the first publication of *The Quiet Rebels*.

Contents

JOSÉ CELSO BARBOSA

CHAPTER 1

Doctor with a Cause

Hermógenes Barbosa was "king of the chimneys." It took a skilled bricklayer to raise a sound wall but building chimneys was something special. Almost everywhere in Bayamón, Hermógenes could point to the fine work of his hands and brain.

There was only one thing wrong with his proud title. He had neither house nor chimney of his own. Queen Isabella II in far-off Spain, yes. She was very rich. But the "king of the chimneys" in Puerto Rico, no. He was poor. So Hermógenes and Carmen Alcalá, his bride of a year, lived in the home of Juan and Lucía Tirado. Juan was his uncle and Lucía was Carmen's sister, older by ten years. It was a good arrangement and not an unusual one for Puerto Rican families. The Tirado couple had no children of their own. The two women had been orphaned when Carmen was only two. From that time onward, Lucía had been mother as much as sister to the younger girl.

Now, on July 27, 1857, there was joy in the house of Tirado and Barbosa. Hermógenes and Carmen had a new son, José Celso. To celebrate his baptism, there was a feast. *Pasteles* (boiled cakes of mashed plantain and meat), *arroz con pollo* (rice and chicken), barbecued pig, cashews, coffee, and rum filled the house with holiday smells. The guests ate, drank, and talked.

The carpenter who sometimes worked with Hermógenes proposed a toast: "To José Celso Barbosa, the
new princeling, who will himself be a king of the chimneys someday." The guests laughed and raised their
glasses. Unsmiling, Lucía Tirado raised hers too. She
drank to the child but not to his chances for fame as
a chimney builder. She had another future in mind for
him. She was determined that the infant Pepito* should
grow up to be "somebody."

In the 1850s, Puerto Rico was a colony ruled by
Spain since Christopher Columbus had landed on the
island some 350 years earlier. When Pepito was born,
about forty-five thousand of Puerto Rico's Negroes
were slaves and about as many were free. His father
and grandfather were free, but even free Negroes had
a hard way to go.

So . . . what were little José's chances? Could he be
a big important landowner or a rich merchant or a
banker? Lucía didn't think so. But there were other
things a man could be, even though he started life poor
and dark-skinned. They, the rich ones, had to respect
the educated ones—the doctors, lawyers, teachers, en-
gineers—and pay for their services. Mamá Lucía promised herself that Pepito would be an educated one. Carmen, Pepito's real mother, was a good mother, but it
was Lucía who did the planning for the whole family.
That's why they called her Mamá Lucía.

Life was hard for most Puerto Ricans. They were
born poor and they died young. In between they had
almost nothing but work and poverty that killed them

---

* Pepito is "little Pepe" and Pepe is the familiar form of José, just as
Bob is used for the name Robert.

before their time. Even the rich were not very rich. Only one out of eleven people could read, and there were very few teachers. To get justice from the government, a poor man, black or white, relied mostly on God. There were very few lawyers, and not many could afford them. Yes, the educated ones were greatly needed in Puerto Rico.

Mamá Lucía's dream for Pepito came close to disaster before the family could begin to follow it. When Pepito was four, his uncle Juan Tirado died. Hermógenes' earnings, and the little tobacco store Juan had left would not be enough to keep the child in school for very long. Lucía grieved and did arithmetic in her head. She sold the tobacco business and the few cattle she kept outside of Bayamón. She bought several small houses to rent. She also became a seamstress, made candy and pastries for stores in San Juan, and cooked complete meals for neighboring families to take home.

The day came when Pepito was big enough to be called Pepe and old enough to sign up in the little school run by Don Olegario Nuñez. The subjects were reading, writing, and Christian doctrine. Having mastered these after several years, Pepe went on to the public school of which Don Gabriel Ferrer Hernández was principal. At home the grownups always found good things to say about Don Gabriel so that Pepe, waiting on his father at mealtime, could hear them.

"He is a truly educated man," Lucía might say. "Much more than most schoolmasters."

"As educated as a Jesuit, and as worthy," Hermógenes could reply. "A man who studied in *Europe!* He is a credit to Bayamón."

"Pepe, what do you think of Don Gabriel?"

"I like him, Mamá Lucía. He helps us when we do not understand something."

"Good! Here, bring your father some more rice. And if you like Don Gabriel so much, then *be* like him."

The boy needed no urging. His head was crowded with questions, big and little. All of them rolled themselves into one big question: "How is the world put together and how do people live in it?" It was not a question to ask of others, but only to be felt inside, like an emptiness in the stomach when he was hungry. It was a hunger for learning and understanding.

On graduation day, the twelve-year-old Pepe received two bronze medals, one for good work, the other for good conduct. Mamá Lucía paid a jeweler to copy them in solid silver.

"We work hard for our money," Hermógenes grumbled. "Why do you spend it as if you were the governor's wife?"

Lucía smiled. "Silver will impress the rector much more than bronze."

"What rector? What are you talking about?"

"We are going to enroll Pepe in the Conciliar Seminary of the priests in San Juan." The seminary was an institution of higher learning open to laymen as well as to candidates for the priesthood.

Hermógenes flung his arms outward in a gesture of disbelief. "Lucía. They have no room there for the likes of us."

"They accepted Baldorioty,* didn't they? A poor boy,

---

* Román Baldorioty de Castro, a Puerto Rican patriot and writer. In 1869 he was elected one of the island's eleven representatives to the Spanish Cortes. He was the founder of Puerto Rico's first Autonomy Party.

whose mother was colored. What's more, she was not married in the church."

"True, but he is very light in color and his father is Spanish. But look at Pepe. They will not want a student whose skin is so dark and whose hair is so tightly curled."

"*Ay bendito*, Hermógenes. If they accepted Baldorioty, they will accept Barbosa! I have done much for the church. I will not be ashamed to remind them."

Mamá Lucía went to San Juan to speak with the rector. She made him look at the silver medals. She told him about Pepe's grandfather, José María Barbosa, a free man who had served the Spanish Crown as a tax collector in the city of Bayamón. Spain had given him a Cross of Merit for preventing bloodshed and making peace when the slaves had rebelled in the little town of Toa Baja. The rector said he would consider admitting the boy.

In 1870, Pepe became the seminary's first Negro student. Since a boy of thirteen could not live by himself in a strange city, Mamá Lucía moved to San Juan with him. Except for her, Pepe led a lonely life. The other students felt they were better than he because of their Spanish blood or their wealthy families. They avoided him. In return, he avoided them. His teachers had to accept him but did little to encourage him. Once the history medal, which he felt he had earned, was awarded to someone else. When he asked why, the teacher made excuses which did not convince young Barbosa.

"*Ay, Padre*," he answered, "I suppose there are differences even in heaven. What a surprise you are going to have when you get there and find you are not sitting right next to the pope."

He could have been expelled for such a remark but he was lucky. At home, Mamá Lucía consoled him: "Don't worry, it's what you know that counts. Nobody can take that away from you."

Since he had no social life, Lucía tried to find other activities he could enjoy. He began to study the flute and the violin. He took long walks. San Juan was an interesting city to explore, but sometimes, when he saw other young people in the streets, his loneliness came back. Once he watched a group of children at play. He noticed especially the oldest girl, a very pretty one, whom the others called Belén. He walked slowly home with her name ringing in his head. He said to himself that one day he would like to marry a girl just like that one. But first he planned to become a lawyer.

In class one day, the teacher asked each of the students what profession he wanted to follow. Barbosa answered *licenciado,* which in Spanish means lawyer. "For sure," the *padre* replied. "You will be a *licenciado de presidio,*" which is the Spanish phrase for a released prisoner. The rest of the class laughed, but the youth had a feeling, somehow, that there would be a time when nobody in San Juan would be able to laugh him off.

At eighteen Barbosa was graduated as a Bachelor of Arts. By now he knew something of the world, and a good deal more about his own green, troubled island. Barbosa's family was well to do compared to the barefooted *jíbaros,* the mountain people who walked or came on skinny horses from their little patches of land to the Bayamón market place. The "free laborers" on the big sugar, coffee, and tobacco plantations were no better off than the *jíbaros*. They were of all colors but none was really free. From 1838 to the early 1860s, harsh laws forced them to work on the plantations for whatever wages, under whatever conditions they were offered. The government repealed the law but it did not repeal their poverty. They continued to work in the fields side by side with the slaves, who often seemed better fed than the free men. In Barbosa's time most Puerto Ricans did not live beyond forty-five. "One does not see many aged people among them," one visitor wrote. "They die off from fevers, contagious diseases and other troubles at a comparatively early age."

Since Puerto Rico was a colony, it was Spain that made the laws. Spain picked the governors, the mayors, and the judges; and Spain supplied the troops to back them up. In the early 1800s, some ideas about changing this type of government began to get around among "the educated ones." They felt Puerto Rico would not improve until it could control its own local affairs. But how?

Some said, "Our rights as Puerto Ricans have to be written into the Spanish Constitution so deep that nothing can erase them." Others said, "*That* will never happen. What we need is complete independence from Spain." Each of these viewpoints had its own group of supporters. And in each group there were many who also said, "We will accomplish nothing until we get rid of slavery."

Most Puerto Ricans spent endless hours in backbreaking work to earn just enough money to keep them alive.

To speak or write boldly and publicly about political change was likely to cost a man some time in jail. It was safe, however, to form an Association for the Abolition of Slavery. By the time Barbosa was born, the ideas of freedom for the slaves, local self-rule, or full independence for Puerto Rico, were growing side by side like three tree trunks held together by the same roots.

In 1868, when Barbosa was only eleven, there was an armed uprising for independence from Spain. In three days, this uprising, *El Grito de Lares* (The Outcry at Lares) was crushed by the governor's troops.

The same year, however, a revolution in Spain overthrew Queen Isabella II. Elections for a new Cortes, Spain's highest lawmaking body, were held in 1869, with Puerto Rico having the right to choose eleven delegates. It was during this election that two definite political parties became established on the island. Those who wanted Spanish rule to continue with no changes at all called themselves the Conservatives. The others, who wanted to increase Puerto Rico's control of its own local affairs, with or without Spain's approval, became the Liberals. The Conservatives elected seven delegates to the Cortes. The Liberals, led by Baldorioty de Castro, elected four. They also won quite a few offices in town and city governments.

In 1873, following another political upheaval, Spain set up a Republican government. The Puerto Rican representatives at the Cortes saw their chance and demanded the full abolition of slavery for their island. Their efforts were successful, and in March of 1873 all remaining slaves in Puerto Rico were freed. Liberals and Conservatives alike were happy to be rid of this unpopular institution.

The Spanish Republic lasted less than a year. King Alfonso XII was placed on the throne and Spain began to tighten control of its colonies. A new governor, General Sanz, was sent to Puerto Rico. Sanz closed down the Liberal newspapers, threw the elected Liberals out of the town governments, and replaced them with Conservatives.

The Conservative triumph was a blow to young Barbosa's plans. Returning to Bayamón from the seminary, he found that his father, being a Liberal, could not get work. Finally Hermógenes did get a job as overseer on a sugar plantation. The owner, Don José Escolástico Berríos, also hired Barbosa as a tutor for his three sons. Impressed by the young man's ability and spirit, the planter offered to help him continue his education. He arranged free passage for Barbosa on a sugar boat to New York and gave him introductions to business friends there. Meanwhile Barbosa took all the English lessons he could from Mary Francis, the Berríos children's other tutor.

On October 19, 1876, he sailed to the great Yankee city to meet the future. But the past is not easily left behind. No one knows this as painfully and lovingly as a young man on his first long journey from home. How would it be to live without Mamá Lucía and Hermógenes and his real mother, Carmen? Did they know how deeply he yearned to thank them for their sacrifices, for the strength they had given him? How hard it is to find the words or the moment for such thanks.

Standing on the deck, he could see San Juan growing smaller in the distance. Setting his face against the threat of tears, he whispered the old affectionate name by which Puerto Ricans call their island, "Borinquen . . ."

His first experiences in New York were encouraging. Attending a private school to improve his English, he was again a Negro student among many whites. Here, however, he made friends. One of them was a doctor who attended Barbosa during an illness. Impressed by the man's skill and kindness, the youth said to him:

"How satisfying it must be to cure people and sometimes to save their lives."

"It's hard work, *amigo*," the medico said, "but I like it. Have you ever considered becoming a doctor yourself?"

"No. At home this would have been impossible for me."

"You are in the United States now. Consider it."

"Thank you. I will think about it very seriously."

The following year Barbosa enrolled at the University of Michigan, in Ann Arbor. He was graduated from medical school, as top-ranking student in his class, in July 1880. He spent several months visiting the hospitals of Washington, D.C., turned down a job in one of them, and returned to Puerto Rico.

During his four years in the United States, Barbosa had learned more than medical science. At Ann Arbor, he had not been scorned for his dark skin or his humble parentage. There, it was able performance and a man's respect for himself that counted. He knew of course

Barbosa graduated from the University of Michigan Medical School as the top-ranking student in his class.

that this was not so in the Southern states, nor in all the Northern ones. He read of lynchings and burned Negro schoolhouses, but also of Negro resistance to discrimination and oppression. He decided that the problems of race and color, like other big social problems, could be solved better under democratic government than under the government of kings. He had studied both systems of politics and government at Ann Arbor. More important, he had lived under both.

Returning to San Juan, he looked up one of his old seminary teachers. *"Buenos días, Padre.* I am Barbosa, formerly one of your students."

"Ciertamente. I remember. What brings you here?"

"I have come to tell you that I have indeed been released, not from the *presidio,* as you prophesied, but from the University of Michigan, with the degree of Doctor of Medicine and Surgery."

"Ah . . . Pepe, my boy! That was a joke. It was meant to challenge you to further study . . ." Joke or not, the *padre's* words had left a scar.

When Barbosa applied for a license to practice medicine in San Juan, he ran into trouble.

"Have you ever studied in Europe?" he was asked.

"No, but I assure you that the University of Michigan is a highly respected institution."

"Among the *norteamericanos,* no doubt. But in San Juan? Impossible. We only accept European degrees."

The young doctor got his license only after the U.S. consul convinced the Spanish governor, Despujols, that Michigan U. had an excellent reputation, even in Europe.

Patients of all classes began to come to Dr. Barbosa.

All had confidence in his ability and the poor were impressed by his kindness. He often gave them money to buy the medicine they needed. His hard work during a smallpox epidemic caused the mayor to name him as a member of the Health Department, but not for long. Higher officials forced the mayor to withdraw the appointment because Barbosa did not have a European degree.

Just the same he was doing well. The number of patients who could afford to pay him and to buy their own medicine grew, though the poor still filled his waiting room. Before many years passed, he was able to bring his family, including Hermógenes, Mamá Lucía, and Carmen, to live with him. He made friends and seemed to be everywhere in San Juan, always helpful, always full of enthusiasm and energy. Maybe he was paying himself back for his earlier years of loneliness.

Everything that had happened to him up to that point made it natural for him to become interested in politics. Invited to give a public lecture in the city of Aguadilla, he chose to speak on the difference between monarchies and republics as forms of government. His talk was interrupted by a message from the military commander of the district ordering him to change his subject. Barbosa ignored it. When the messenger came back with a second warning the doctor handed him a calling card and said:

"Tell your chief I will meet him on the field of honor whenever he wishes." There were no further interruptions. Nor was Barbosa's challenge to a duel ever accepted. The doctor was an expert swordsman and made no secret of the fact. Though he never fought a duel himself, he was often chosen as a second by other duelists, which was a sign of great respect. Once he seconded his fellow Liberal, Luis Muñoz Rivera, in a famous duel with the Conservative Vicente Balbás Capó.

There was a happier adventure, too. One evening he was called to the bedside of a young woman. He asked her questions and gave her some medicine, staring at her meanwhile in the dim light of the room's only lamp. She reminded him of someone—but of whom? Promising to return the next day, Dr. Barbosa left the house far more upset than his patient.

"Her name? Her name? Why did I not ask it? *Dios!* Is it possible that this is the young girl, Belén, whom I once saw playing on the street so long ago, when I was in the seminary?" There would be a simple way to find out, if this night would ever end.

Entering her room the next morning, he said, "Good morning, Belén. How do you feel?"

She answered, "Good morning, Doctor. It hurts less today."

He had found her! He made certain he would never lose her again. Dr. Barbosa and Belén Sanchez were married on June 9, 1885. His family approved wholeheartedly. After the wedding, Mamá Lucía handed the household keys to the bride. Belén refused them. She begged the older woman to remain mistress of the household and to treat her as a daughter.

Lucía Tirado's death in 1888 and Carmen Barbosa's a year later cut short the time in which both women could enjoy Pepe's successes and their family's good fortune.

Puerto Rico as a whole, however, was not so fortunate.

Those were gloomy times. Like General Sanz, the governors who followed him saw to it that the Conservatives held all the power. When there were elections, the Conservatives controlled them. They said who could vote; they counted the votes, and they said who won the election, whether they did or not. The Liberal Party began to go to pieces, but the ones who meant business stuck together the best way they could.

One day a leader of the Conservatives said to Barbosa, "You know, Doctor, it's nice to have a sensible man like you around, who does not get mixed up in antigovernment politics." To a Conservative, anyone who wanted to change anything in Puerto Rico was "against the government."

That did it. Barbosa, who belonged to neither party, joined the Liberal Reform Party the next day. He began to attend the discussions in the back of Del Valle's drugstore, a Liberal hangout in San Juan.

The Liberals did not want to break away from Spain. All they wanted was some form of self-government for Puerto Rico. Most of them thought all would be well if the island were made a province, with the same rights as the provinces of Spain itself. They expressed this idea in the word *assimilation*, which means "making or becoming the same as."

To Barbosa, the idea of assimilation did not mean much, because Spain did not have a republican form of government. "None of the provinces have any real freedom," he pointed out. "Spain is a monarchy. Almost anything can be done there in the name of the king. So what good is assimilation?"

Barbosa did not want independence either. He did

want a Puerto Rican government which could make decisions and pass laws on local matters without interference from the government in Spain. The political word for this kind of freedom is *autonomy,* which means "self-management." With autonomy Puerto Ricans could set up their own republican government.

More and more people began to see the situation as Barbosa saw it. To reorganize the Liberals, Baldorioty de Castro called a big conference in the city of Ponce in March 1887. Barbosa was chosen as one of the delegates from San Juan. The Spanish authorities grew very nervous about the meeting. The word went out that anyone who attended might be thrown into jail. Barbosa's family asked him not to go.

"I must," he answered.

"What about your patients, your career, your family?"

"It is my duty," he muttered, and he went.

The meeting worked out a statement of its political ideas, the Ponce Plan, which backed up much of Barbosa's thinking. Then the Liberals reorganized themselves as the Autonomist Party. While in Ponce, Barbosa also joined a secret group, *Sociedad Torre del Viejo* (Society of the Old Man's Tower). Its aim was to help native Puerto Ricans get a fair share of the island's business action. Since there was no well-developed banking system from which Puerto Ricans could get business loans, the society members used their own money to set up Puerto Rican-owned, pro-Autonomist businesses. They conducted a quiet boycott, refusing to deal with Conservative-owned enterprises. In a short time this "buy Puerto Rican" movement began to make itself felt all over the island.

Governor Palacio gave a harsh answer to the Ponce conference and the boycott. Liberal leaders, including Baldorioty, were imprisoned in El Morro fortress, whether they belonged to the Old Man's Tower or not. To Palacio they all seemed the same. Jails across the island held hundreds of others. There were beatings and torture. The police had spies everywhere. Whole families slept in the woods for fear of a policeman's midnight knock on the door. Rumors began to circulate that the prisoners in El Morro would be shot.

Barbosa, however, was not arrested. The police did not think they could get away with it. Some of his patients were important Conservatives. They would complain about losing their family doctor.

Outgoing mail and cablegrams were carefully censored to keep the rest of the world from knowing about Palacio's reign of terror. No one was allowed to leave the island without police permission. Among those who did manage to get out was Juan Arrillaga Roque. He reached Spain with a report of what was happening. Just when things were at their worst, the news came that the king had agreed to send a new governor to replace Palacio.

Dr. Barbosa immediately thought of a way to let the prisoners know they would soon be free. Early in the morning he went to El Morro, explaining that he had to attend the sick wife of the military commander. A sergeant escorted him to the lady's bedside. On the way, he stopped at Baldorioty's jail cell and told him the good news. Soon the message spread from man to man: "Palacio is finished. The new governor will let us go." It was true. But the year of 1887 is still known in Puerto Rican history as *El Año Terrible*, "The Terrible Year."

Afterward, although Puerto Rican feeling against Spain became stronger than ever, the Autonomist Party was too weak to do anything. Many of its leaders had fled from the island. Some went to Cuba to help José Martí's Cuban independence movement. Some just gave up. Baldorioty, the man who held the party together, died in 1889.

Barbosa did not quit. He stuck to politics, took care of his patients, and was invited to become a professor of natural history in the Puerto Rico Athenaeum. First, though, he had to take an examination to prove he knew enough to teach medical subjects. Even though he was one of the best-known doctors on the island, his degree of M.D. from the University of Michigan had never been officially recognized. The Spanish board of examiners tried to make it impossible for him. One of them refused to wear his official robes to interview a Negro. The others "put him on" with insultingly simple high school questions. Some of Barbosa's friends walked out in protest, but the doctor remained calm. They *had* to certify him, and they knew it. He remained a working member of the Athenaeum faculty for twelve years, until 1902.

After the death of Baldorioty, three men stood out as leaders of the Autonomist Party: Luis Muñoz Rivera, José de Diego and José Celso Barbosa. All three agreed that Puerto Rico ought to be self-governing. But the same old arguments that divided the Liberals in earlier years kept coming up again.

What kind of self-government? How should they try to get it? Each man had his own ideas. Muñoz Rivera was willing to work with the Monarchist parties in Spain in order to gain some form of autonomy. Barbosa insisted that it was a mistake to do business with any political groups in Spain except those who wanted to make Spain a republic. De Diego wanted to work steadily but peacefully for Puerto Rico's total independence. He approved of autonomy only as a step toward independence. In the meantime, he agreed with Muñoz Rivera that one should work in Spain with whichever party was willing to grant self-government to the island. There were others, not many, who wanted to fight for the island's independence with guns if necessary, as the thirteen North American colonies had to do before they could form the United States.

Year after year these conflicting groups within the Autonomist Party went on arguing. They were hitched to a wagonload of hopes that did not move because they could not agree on which direction to pull it.

In 1894 Barbosa was chosen as one of the Autonomist Party's directorate. In less than a year they formed new local committees all over the island and raised a campaign fund for a coming election contest with the Conservatives. The Autonomist candidates won important offices in several parts of Puerto Rico and showed some real strength for the first time in many years. Two were elected as the island's delegates to the Cortes.

Nevertheless, the conflict between Barbosa and Muñoz Rivera continued. It grew worse when Muñoz went to Spain and came back reporting that Práxedes

Mateo Sagasta, a liberal-monarchist politician, had promised to give Puerto Rico a very favorable Charter of Autonomy as soon as he became Prime Minister.

Sagasta kept his promise. The new charter went into effect in December 1897. It gave Puerto Rico equality with the other provinces in Spain itself. It also permitted the local political parties to elect the chief officers of the island's government as well as a legislature with real lawmaking powers. There would still be a governor, appointed by Spain, but he would be more of an ambassador now, and much less of a one-man ruler.

Defeated, Barbosa still refused to believe in what he considered to be a false autonomy, "false" because of its connections with the monarchy. He withdrew from the party of Muñoz, and he and his followers became known as *puros*.

The guns of eight U.S. warships, firing at San Juan on May 12, 1898 drowned out all political bickering for a while. When Dr. Barbosa, in Bayamón that day, heard them, his first thought was, "If they are shooting at the city there may be dead and wounded. I've got to get back, *pronto*. They'll need me at the hospital." To go all the way by land would take many hours. Instead he rode his horse at a gallop three miles to Cataño. There he borrowed a boat and pulled at the oars for a mile and a half across the bay while U. S. Navy shells whistled overhead. He made it to a San Juan dock, with sailors on the Spanish ships in the harbor cheering his puny rowboat home. Then he rushed to his post at the hospital.

Taking the shortest route to the hospital, Dr. Barbosa rowed a mile and a half across the bay as U. S. Navy shells whistled overhead.

Barbosa admired the United States but he felt that its war against Spain was wrong. *El Pais,** a *puro* newspaper of which he was editor, said the North Americans were not being true to their ideals. He also supported the Spanish war effort as a district chief medical officer of the Red Cross in San Juan. In August, when Spain surrendered and Puerto Rico became a United States possession, Dr. Barbosa no longer felt that he ought to hold back on his pro-U.S. sympathies.

Maybe now, at last, Puerto Rico could have its own truly republican kind of government. Maybe the way would be open, quickly, to more and better schools, houses, hospitals, roads, and jobs for all who had been without them. Surely the United States, so proud of its democracy, would not begrudge Puerto Ricans the right to run their own lives and their own homeland.

In mid-October 1898, the *puros'* top leaders met at Barbosa's house to discuss the island's future. They decided they wanted Puerto Rico to become "a territory today and a state of the Union tomorrow." At that time the *puros* also changed their name to the Republican Party. But it was the Congress of the North American giant and not the Puerto Ricans who decided what kind of government they would have. Under the Foraker Act† a governor was appointed by the President of the U.S. A legislative assembly with two "houses" was set up. One was an elected thirty-five-man Chamber of Delegates. The other was an Executive Council of eleven men appointed by the U. S. President. Under the law

* *The Nation.*

† Introduced by Senator Joseph B. Foraker, Republican, from Ohio. It became a law April 12, 1900.

five members of the Executive Council had to be Puerto
Ricans. The six others were North Americans. The
Foraker Act was a disappointment to the Puerto Ricans.
It gave them less power than they had under the Spanish 1897 Charter of Autonomy. Since it was the best
deal they could get they were willing to wait and
see. . . .

Dr. Barbosa, chosen as a member of the Executive
Council, became one of a dozen men in positions of the
highest authority Puerto Ricans were allowed to hold.
The first meeting of the Legislative Assembly was called
in the large theater in San Juan's Plaza de Colón (Columbus Square). Two thousand people attended the
opening ceremonies in a holiday mood. The auditorium
was filled with the scent of flowers, the dazzle of flags,
the rousing music of two bands, and the hope of better
times ahead.

The new chamber passed a number of good laws.
Dr. Barbosa was especially active in supporting a bill of
rights similar to the first ten amendments in the U. S.
Constitution. Remembering his own opportunity for education in New York and Michigan, he put through a
law to give scholarships to Puerto Rican students in
United States colleges. Dr. Barbosa was the only council
member to be appointed five times in a row. He served
from 1900 until 1917, when the council was abolished
by the Jones Act. *El Bill Jones,* as the Puerto Ricans
called it, was passed by the U. S. Congress to replace
the Foraker Act. Instead of an Executive Council
named by the President, there was a Senate elected by
the people of the island. This, together with a new
House of Representatives, made up the Legislature of

Puerto Rico. Dr. Barbosa was elected to the Senate in 1917 and again in 1920.

In one way the new law made Barbosa feel he had been on the right track from the beginning. It made all Puerto Ricans citizens of the United States and put them directly under the protection of the U. S. Constitution. In another way, he was dissatisfied with *El Bill Jones,*

"We now enjoy under the American flag the same political rights as any other Americans," he wrote. "But economically we have advanced very little. One cannot say one controls a country if one does not control its wealth. Puerto Ricans! Work constantly with one purpose only—to recover our lands and be the sole owners of our country!"

Actually, Barbosa and Muñoz Rivera were no longer very far apart in their ideas of what was best for Puerto Rico. Yet the political conflict between the *Barbosistas* and the *Muñocistas* continued. Neither side was pleased with the treatment Puerto Rico was receiving from the United States. Yet neither side really believed that Puerto Rico, small, poor, defenseless, could make it as an independent country. Muñoz said that he favored independence at some future time but that first Puerto Rico must work for more self-government in co-operation with the United States. Barbosa was flatly against independence. Puerto Rico must become a state, he insisted. This would give his people the highest independence they could ever expect, which was not bad, in his opinion, because it would make them equal with all other North Americans.

At sixty-four, Dr. Barbosa, serving his second term

as a senator-at-large, was practicing less medicine and more politics. He was generally recognized as the real leader of the Republican Party but he refused to be its official chief. He feared it would hurt the party for a Negro to accept the title. This might seem strange thinking for a man as courageous and proud as Barbosa, but his fears were real.

Election campaigns were rough. Candidates for office could not disagree very much about the real issues because everybody knew what Puerto Rico needed. Still poverty-ridden, despite U.S. rule, it needed a double helping of everything; and first of all it needed to get out from under the control of the big U.S. sugar companies. But anything went when a speaker faced an audience or when an editorial writer stared at a blank sheet of paper. Campaigners were likely to attack not only an opponent's political beliefs but his honesty, intelligence, morals, ancestry, and personal appearance. Barbosa's dark skin did not keep him from having a wide, many-colored circle of personal and political friends. Nevertheless, his political enemies tried to hurt him by speaking of him as "the Negro, Barbosa." Barbosa's enemies wrote to the newly elected U. S. President to remind him that Barbosa was a Negro and therefore should not be reappointed to the Executive Council of Puerto Rico. Theodore Roosevelt, William Howard Taft and Woodrow Wilson preferred to remember that he was one of the most powerful and able leaders on the island. They kept reappointing him. They knew that Barbosa was not the leader of a Negro party but of a political party in which people of many colors participated freely, according to their personal

interests and beliefs. The same was true of the other
parties and their leaders.

In Puerto Rico color did make some difference in
people's private social lives. In politics it was a phony
issue. But because it kept coming up, Dr. Barbosa wrote
a newspaper article on the subject every once in a while.
The articles were later collected in a book called *Pro-
blemas de Raza* (Problems of Race). The nitty-gritty of
his writings on the subject was this:

"Black, black, black! I am proud of being Negro . . . ! Nor have I ever tried to beg tolerance
from anyone . . . Rather, I am comfortable with the
adjective . . . The colored man in Puerto Rico has con-
tributed and is contributing, with his actions, to the
prestige of our race and the country of our birth. Su-
periority is not proved by color . . . but by the number
of connecting links in the brain, by education, by will-
power, by moral courage."

Early in 1921 the tireless Barbosa felt tired. He
shrugged it off. "I'm getting old, that's all." Speaking on
the subject of independence versus statehood in the
Senate on May 30, he did not seem old or tired but it
was his last speech. He knew by then that he had
cancer. So did his nine living sons and daughters. Gui-
llermo, a surgeon, returned from Paris. Young Manolo,
a journalism student, hurried home from Washington.
To him, Dr. Barbosa said, "Go back to school, son. It
may take me months to die. Meanwhile you'll be losing
a lot of time here. We'll keep you posted." The others
were close at hand: Lucía, a schoolteacher; Pedro Juan;
Francisco; Roberto, a dentist; Pilar, who wrote of his
life and work; Rafael, a lawyer and a member of the

Puerto Rico House of Representatives. And there was Carmen Belén, the first-born, unmarried, a talented pianist of concert stage caliber. She often played for him in the evenings while passersby stopped under their windows to listen. In those last months it seemed to him that she played more beautifully than ever.

In September he agreed to undergo surgery but said he would prefer to have it done at home. It was his polite way of telling his fellow doctors, "I know it's hopeless, so why not let me die in my own bed?" He obliged them, however, by showing up at the hospital, smiling: "Doctors, I promised to come and here I am. But I warn you, this is the last promise I will keep." He died on September 21, 1921.

To all of his countrymen, the facts and the deeds of his life still say:

We were descendants of European conquerors, Indian natives, and transported Africans. None of us is one or another of these three any more. We are Puerto Ricans! We have become a *people,* with our own past, our own traditions, our own "national" personality. We must choose for ourselves how we want Puerto Rico to live with the rest of the world!

LUIS MUÑOZ RIVERA

CHAPTER 2

The Man on the Mountain

At daybreak voices in the street awakened the mayor. They were singing *alboradas*, the early morning carols that begin the feast days of saints. And today Barranquitas, a village in the central highlands of Puerto Rico, was honoring the Virgin of Carmel.

Don Luis Muñoz Barrios smiled as he listened. He knew what kind of a day this would be. During Mass, in the wooden church with the sheet-iron roof, the *alboradores* would sing again to the beat of guitars, castanets, *güiros*. There would be cockfights and sack races in the plaza. Little stands would sell fried fish, *chicharrones* (hog cracklings), mangoes, and star apples, to be washed down with *mabí*, *horchata*, and other fruit drinks. The *jíbaros* (country people) would outdo each other in making up *décimas* (folk songs) on the spot. After dark everyone would dance the *seis*, a lively free-swinging country dance.

Early that evening Don Luis strolled about the plaza to see and be seen, to greet people and be greeted. It was expected of him. Then he turned home again to wait, as he had waited all week, for his young wife, Doña Monserrate, to give birth to their first child. It happened the next day.

Luis Muñoz Rivera was born July 17, 1859. At six, his parents sent him to the only school in Barranquitas.

At ten, having outgrown and outstudied the small school, he turned to private tutors. His father, no longer mayor, but still a merchant, landowner, and the town's notary public, taught him bookkeeping. The years of Luis's growing up were also years of a great political debate about Puerto Rico's relations with Spain. In his own family his father and his uncle, Don Vicente Muñoz Barrios, argued endlessly about it.

"The trouble is," Don Vicente might say, "that we are not making either Spain or ourselves rich."

"And whose fault is that, Brother?"

"It is the fault of history. For 350 years our island was little more than a naval base for Spain to use in protecting her richer colonies."

"We played a worthy role," Don Luis might answer. "We guarded Spanish civilization in the New World, and now—doesn't the new constitution of 1869 show that Spain really does care about us?"

"We have had other constitutions, Luis, in 1812, 1837, 1845. They come and go."

"But there were eleven Puerto Ricans in the Cortes* which wrote this one. We ourselves elected them only last year in a free election. Four of them, led by your Baldorioty de Castro, spoke for such liberals as you, Vicente. Seven of them spoke for me and the other conservatives. As a result, we now have political parties for the first time in Puerto Rico's history. Do these events mean nothing?"

* The highest Spanish legislature, made up of delegates from all the provinces of Spain. Similar to the U. S. Congress as a nation-wide body, but different in its powers. By law, it was subject to the will of the ruling king or queen.

As a young boy, Luis listened to his father and uncle argue endlessly about Puerto Rico's future.

"They mean much. But our Spanish governors still hold the real power. In thirty-five years we have had sixteen of them, some good, some bad. We cannot plan for the future because what one governor approves the next one may forbid. And so, year after year, Puerto Rico lives like a poor relation in the family of Spain."

"Nonsense. When we appeal to Madrid, the mistakes are corrected."

"Yes, if Madrid, which has other troubles, has time to think about us."

"What would you want instead, Vicente? Independence?"

"No! Autonomy! The right of Puerto Ricans to decide all matters which are purely Puerto Rican."

"Will you admit, at least, that in the past two years we have taken a great step forward?"

"Certainly, but we must see where it leads."

The arguments interested young Luis. He, too, wanted to see where it would all lead. For a few years, the island seemed well on its way to getting what Uncle Vicente wanted. Puerto Rico was allowed to have a legislature of its own, called the Provincial Assembly. It had some authority, but not much, over budgets, taxes, and appointments to office. Puerto Rico sent fourteen Liberals and only one Conservative to the Cortes of 1873. The Cortes proclaimed Spain a republic and through the efforts of the Puerto Rican members abolished slavery on the island.

The republic was overthrown a year later and Spain came under the rule of royalty again. General Sanz, once recalled from Puerto Rico for his harsh treatment of the Liberals, became governor again. He dissolved the Provincial Assembly and "fired" all the Liberals in the town governments. The Conservatives, with Sanz's powerful help, kept them down. Puerto Ricans settled back for a long stretch of one-party government, but, having had a taste of Spanish liberalism, they wanted more.

Meanwhile Luis still had some growing up to do. His mother died when he was twelve. Soon after, he took on the job of tutoring his nine younger brothers. At fourteen he tended store and copied legal documents for his father. He continued his education alone, using the hundreds of Spanish and French books in his father's library. By sixteen he had read a great deal about politics, though he planned to be a writer, especially of poetry. In his free time he wrote and wrote but kept his work to himself until he felt sure it was good enough to send out.

He did not see himself in print until 1882. When he was twenty-five, a newspaper in Ponce, *El Pueblo* (The People), published his poem *Adelante* (Forward!). Mario Braschi, the editor, encouraged him but wrote: "I hope you will not start composing all sorts of love poems. Today a poet must express the spirit that moves men toward science, liberty, betterment . . ." Well, that was the way young Luis Muñoz felt about it too:

> I was not born to sing pretty songs
> Like a captive nightingale.
> I am going to rough and unknown regions.
> I will reach my journey's end
> with broken wings; but I will arrive.

In 1883 he joined the Barranquitas Liberal Party.

A year later Muñoz and his boyhood friend, Quintín Negrón Sanjurjo, opened a little general store. Beans and calico went for cash. Discussion of Puerto Rico's problems was free.

What were these problems? Salvador Brau, one of the island's most respected thinkers, who was also editor of *El Clamor de País* (The Cry of the Country), described them this way:

> Without schools; without books whose importation is forbidden by the Customs; without newspapers whose circulation is suppressed; without political representation, without municipal self-government, the physical and mental energies of the people are entirely taken up in the production of sugar to sell to England and the United States. Puerto Rico is simply a factory openly exploited.

Muñoz and Brau belonged to the small class who had education, money, and a chance to be somebody. But to men with their qualities, *being* somebody meant *doing* something. And to them, the biggest job worth doing was to improve life, at least a little, for all Puerto Ricans. Without that, even the *somebodies* would stop amounting to much.

Though the party hardly existed in 1885, Muñoz ran for the Provincial Assembly as a Liberal. He lost the election. Then, in January 1887, the party held a conference at Coamo to reorganize the movement. Muñoz was president of the Barranquitas Committee. Called upon to speak, unexpectedly, he rose and smiled.

"Since I am not prepared to make any organizational or political proposals at this moment, I beg your leave to read one of my poems."

"Read it! By all means!" voices cried out. His poem spoke of hope, of struggle, of faith in his people and his homeland. The applauding listeners were as much impressed by the poet as by his poem. It was here that he first met Román Baldorioty de Castro, "elder statesman" of the liberal movement. In Ponce, on March 7, 1887, the Liberals and their sympathizers held another, much larger, meeting. It was attended by delegates from the island's seventy-one towns who voted to form the Autonomist Party. The new party took up where the Liberal Party, no longer in existence, had left off. Baldorioty introduced Muñoz to his friends, spoke of him as "my disciple," and said, "I think he will continue our work when we are gone."

The Autonomist Party grew quickly. This alarmed the Conservatives. They accused it of being a "front" for a supposedly terrorist society called "The Old Man's Tower." (Actually the tower was just a "buy Puerto Rican, hire Puerto Ricans" movement.) Town officials secretly sent lists of "disloyal" Autonomists to General Palacio, the new governor. The mayor of Barranquitas wrote that Muñoz Rivera was a leader in a dangerous group called *El Corazón Negro* (The Black Heart), the existence of which was never really proved.

Palacio, believing these tales or not, declared martial law, which meant military dictatorship. He ordered the arrest of Baldorioty and four hundred others. A storm of protest broke out in the Autonomist newspapers. Editors who reported the torture, beating, and mistreatment of prisoners found themselves arrested. Salvador Brau of *El Clamor* was released on bail. Ramón Marín, of *El Pueblo*, with a gun at his head, had to promise that he would publish an apology for "lying." (He closed up shop instead.) Francisco Cepeda, editor and owner of *La Revista* (The Review), was questioned, beaten, and thrown in a cell. A friend wrote to Muñoz:

"The paper is closing. Come to Ponce and take over for this heroic editor. There is danger, but no matter . . ."

Muñoz replied: "I am willing. I know the possible consequences and I accept them." But the paper had to shut down to protect Cepeda from further harm in prison.

Palacio tried to keep complaints about him from reaching Madrid. Autonomists caught leaving the island were arrested. The news got back to Spain anyhow and in November 1887 the governor was recalled to Madrid. The prisoners were released, but *El Año Terrible* (The Terrible Year) left the Autonomist forces in bad shape. Quarrels broke out among the leaders. Baldorioty, ill and old, resigned as the party's president.

In the 1889 election for Provincial Assembly delegates, the Autonomists chose Luis Muñoz Rivera as their candidate in two districts, Caguas and Juana Díaz. Then the Conservatives announced that his father, Luis Muñoz Barrios, would be *their* candidate in Juana Díaz. An impossible situation! Out of respect for his father, young Luis quit the Juana Díaz contest. Out of respect for his beliefs, he campaigned for Manuel Rossy, his father's new opponent. Rossy won. So did young Muñoz in Caguas, but he never took office because his election was challenged. By the time the courts decided in his favor, his term had run out.

The death of Román Baldorioty on September 30,

1889, left the Autonomists without a leader. At the funeral service, there was a telegram from Muñoz Rivera:

"Something very close to my heart has been stolen away. To whom shall we go now for advice? Who has his generosity of heart, the gravity and kindness of his character, the steady light of his exceptional intelligence?" When Ramón Marín heard the sender's name, he exclaimed, "There is the man of the future!" All over the room heads nodded in agreement.

Leadership was not handed to Muñoz gift-wrapped. He had to win it. Early in 1890 he sold his share in Muñoz & Negrón and borrowed additional money to set up a weekly newspaper in Ponce. Ramón Marín helped him open his office.

The first issue of *La Democracia*, July 1, 1890, made the paper and its editor famous on the island almost overnight. Muñoz's writing style made his readers *feel* as well as understand. Most of his articles were about subjects that affected the daily lives of Puerto Ricans. Time and again the government hauled him into court for violating the newspaper censorship laws. Once he spent two days in jail, until his father put up 15,000 pesetas for bond.

La Democracia gave new hope to the Autonomists and new life to an old argument about two ways of giving Puerto Ricans control of their local government. One was *assimilation*, which would guarantee Puerto Rico's full rights as a Spanish province.[*] The other was

---

[*] The provinces of Spain are large territorial divisions such as the states making up the U.S. That would have made Puerto Rico an overseas province just as Hawaii is an overseas state.

autonomy, a type of self-government which would enable the island to handle its own special problems in its own way. This did not mean full independence from Spain. Under autonomy Puerto Rico would live in a commonwealth arrangement with Spain, such as Canada still has with Great Britain.

This debate, which started in 1887, was still going on in May 1891, when Muñoz and his paper demanded action to secure autonomy:

"We are too weak. An alliance with a political party in Spain will make us strong."

Another Autonomist leader, José Celso Barbosa, listened.

"Which political party?" he asked.

"The Liberal Fusion Party led by Práxedes Mateo Sagasta."

"They're monarchists!" Barbosa cried. "And they are not the ruling party now. Besides, Puerto Rico has always done better when Spain was ruled by republican parties."

Muñoz answered: "They are *liberal* monarchists. And Sagasta has more chance of taking power than any republican. When he does, both partners will benefit—autonomy for Puerto Rico, and Autonomist votes in the Cortes for Sagasta's administration."

"Never!" said Barbosa and his followers. "Sagasta will give us nothing or very little. Only a *republican* Spanish party will give Puerto Rico the kind of freedom it needs."

This new quarrel went on for four years, with Muñoz shouting his weekly battle cries in *La Democracia*—against the Conservatives, the other Autonomists, and

the Spanish regime. Off duty he spoke in gentler tones
to Amalia Marín, daughter of his friend and political
ally. She said "yes" and they were married in Ponce
Cathedral in 1893.

In 1895, the Conservatives still had everything going
their way. The Autonomists, though gaining popularity,
were still weak. Tired of seeing nothing happen, Muñoz sailed to Spain to study the political situation there
on his own. He returned in January 1896 convinced
that there was no use in trying to keep the Autonomist
Party alive unless it really accepted an alliance with
Sagasta's party in Spain. He knew he would face a
bitter battle with José Barbosa's followers on this point
at the upcoming convention. But before the convention, he had a personal sword duel to fight with Balbás
Capó, a leading Conservative.

Angered by an article in *La Democracia,* Balbás had
issued a challenge good for any "responsible" staff member. Muñoz said, "It's my paper. I'm responsible." He
invited Dr. Barbosa, his enemy in party councils, but a
personal friend, to be his second. Balbás, an expert
swordsman, had the reputation of dueling for keeps.
But Muñoz left the field with only a slight wound
because his pen was mightier than Balbás Capó's sword.
Balbás understood that to kill the editor of *La Democracia* could make him the most hated and maybe the
most hunted man in Puerto Rico.

The *Muñocistas,* and the *Barbosistas,* finally did agree
at the convention to send four men including Muñoz
to Spain to find the best political ally they could. They
arrived there late in the year 1896. Muñoz was right:

Sagasta was the only Spanish leader who was interested. But in a private talk with Muñoz he said:

"What will you do if we can't work out an agreement?"

"I will stop off in New York on my way home," the Puerto Rican replied.

New York was headquarters for a small group which was trying to form a Puerto Rican liberation army. With a revolutionary war against Spain already going in Cuba, Muñoz's threat meant something.

"Don Luis," said Sagasta, "may I offer you one of these cigars? Excellent tobacco—grown on your beautiful island."

The delegation went straight home. At the Autonomist convention of February 1897, they presented the agreement they had made with Sagasta. The agreement was this. If and when Sagasta became prime minister, he would do everything in his power to see that Spain granted Puerto Rico a Charter of Autonomy. It was clear, of course, that in return the Autonomist Party would support Sagasta and his followers in Spanish politics. The Sagasta Pact, for which Muñoz had campaigned for six years, was adopted by a large majority vote. Immediately, Dr. Barbosa and his group walked out, still wanting no gifts from monarchist hands. They named themselves the Orthodox Autonomist Party and were known as *puros*. The Muñoz wing became the Liberal Party. There would be political war between the two for years to come.

Muñoz had picked a winner. Sagasta became prime minister in August. Puerto Rico received its Charter of Autonomy in December. A six-man Executive Council

Muñoz, as editor of La Democracia, *accepted the challenge of a duel with Balbás.*

of cabinet rank was formed at once—three *Liberales* and three *Ortodoxos*. Muñoz, one of the six, had the title of Secretary of Grace,* Justice and Government. It was the most important post in the council.

General elections for the new island legislature and for hundreds of local offices were held in March 1898. There would still be a governor appointed by Spain but with greatly reduced authority.

"Now the idea of autonomy is no longer a dream," said Muñoz. "Our party is no longer a propaganda group; it is now the party of government."

But even as he spoke, he knew that Spain's time in Puerto Rico, with or without autonomy, was running out. In April the United States and Spain were at war. In May, U.S. warships bombarded San Juan. If the North Americans came, Muñoz wanted them to find the new government in full operation. That would be one way of putting them on notice that Puerto Rico needed no outside help in running its affairs. Both branches of the island legislature began their first sessions on July 18. And Muñoz became the head of a new Executive Council. They were still at it on July 25, when U. S. Army troops landed at Guánica, seventy miles away. What would become of Puerto Rico's self-government now?

A truce signed on August 12 placed the island completely under U.S. military control. Muñoz, Spanish in blood, bone, and spirit, did not welcome the English-speaking Americans as Puerto Rico's overlords. He cer-

* The word Grace was used to show that mercy and justice always belong together. The minister could issue pardons, paroles, etc.

tainly did not want to be a secretary of government
taking orders from a conquering army. He retired to
Barranquitas with Doña Amalia and their infant son,
the third Luis Muñoz.

He felt like Sisyphus in the ancient Greek legend.
Sisyphus was doomed forever to push a huge rock up
the side of a steep mountain—an endless task because
the rock kept slipping back. It had seemed to be an
idle story when he first read it but now . . . "Yes, of
course . . ."

His pen moved broodingly across the paper . . . His
Sísifo was not just the ancient Greek folk tale retold in
Spanish. It was the story of what had happened to his
country, and to him. In Muñoz's poem, Sisyphus *suc-
ceeds* but then "a slight tremor arises from the north,"
the mountain trembles, and the rock rolls down again:

> In this, the bitter symbol of our sterile strife,
> Behold, entire, the story of the poet's life.

Well, that was the way the earth shook. He *was*
Sisyphus, and it was time to get on up the mountain
again. Returning to San Juan, he tried to resign. However, he and the rest of his cabinet remained in office
at the request of the military governor, General John R.
Brooke. But Luis Muñoz Rivera, the cultured Puerto
Rican gentleman, and Guy V. Henry, the rough-and-
ready general who replaced Brooke, were unable to get
along. In one of their many stormy business meetings,
General Henry said to the interpreter:

"Tell Muñoz I'm sick of hearing him argue about
every decision I make. So far I haven't lost my temper

When Puerto Rico fell under U.S. military control, Muñoz retired to
Barranquitas with his wife and infant son.

but I've knocked down bigger men than him."

Muñoz's eyes covered Henry with frost. Turning to the interpreter, he said, "Please inform the general that if he undertakes to behave violently toward me, I will be obliged to throw him out of the window." End of business meeting. Early in 1899, Muñoz resigned.

The island sugar growers then asked him to go to Washington. They wanted to make sure that the federal trade and tax laws would give them equal treatment with the sugar growers of Louisiana and the West. Because, if anything happened to prevent Puerto Rico from selling most of its sugar crop to the United States, there would be hard times all over the island. To pay for all his expenses, they gave him a letter of credit allowing him to draw whatever money he wished from a Washington bank account. Muñoz, however, valued his own autonomy as much as his homeland's. When he returned to the island, he handed back the letter of credit, unused.

Muñoz had seen and felt the good will of the American people. He now believed that the big busy republic of the north could be lived with. So did Dr. Barbosa, pro-American since he was a medical student at the University of Michigan. The political parties of both men wanted much the same things: an end to military government, a quick switch-over from Spanish to U.S. money; free trade (no import taxes) between the island and the mainland; federal loans for sugar, coffee, and tobacco farming, ruined by the hurricane of August 8, 1899. Both expected Puerto Rico to be, first, an organized territory and, later, a state.

In San Juan, where the government was located,

In one of Muñoz's arguments with the military governor he said, "Please inform the general that if he undertakes to behave violently toward me, I will be obliged to throw him out of the window."

Muñoz put out the first issue of his party's new paper, *El Diario* (The Journal) on January 5, 1900. In April, Congress passed the Foraker Bill, as the official rule book for Puerto Rican government. Charles H. Allen, the first civilian governor, saw a difference between the attitudes of the two parties toward U.S. authority over their island. The *Barbosistas,** who changed their name to the Republican Party, welcomed it sincerely as a step in the right direction, though they were not entirely happy with it. The *Muñocistas,†* now called the Federal Party, took it like medicine, making faces about the taste.

The Puerto Rican summer of 1900 was made hot by the election campaign for a new thirty-five-man Chamber of Delegates. From both camps, a heavy smog of political and personal name-calling rose over San Juan. In September, after *El Diario* printed an editorial "blasting" the Republican mayor of San Juan, a mob wrecked its office and printing press. When Muñoz's friends heard that "the word was out" for him, they formed a bodyguard. At his doorway in the evening, they found a group of strangers waiting. There were angry shouts, followed by pistol shots. No one was hit. The police made no effort to find the leaders of the other group, but Muñoz and his friends were arrested for armed assault. When they came up for trial, the judge asked Muñoz if he had ever before been charged with breaking the law.

"Forty-two times," the editor replied. "And every time it was for wanting to make a free country out of

* Barbosa's supporters.
† Muñoz's supporters.

what others want to turn into a slave colony; the same
as now, Your Honor." All were acquitted.

Two days before the election, the *Federales* pulled
out of the race. They charged that the rules gave them
no protection against being cheated out of thousands
of votes at the polling places. The result was a clean
sweep for the *Republicanos*, and the tables were turned.
The *Federales*, who had been "in" with Sagasta and
General Brooke, were "out" now. Many of them blamed
Muñoz, even though he had advised them against boy-
cotting the election. The rock, the great, crushing rock,
was forcing him downhill again. He needed a better
footing. . . .

He retreated to Caguas and reopened *La Democracia*,
putting a trusted editor in charge. Then he moved to
New York. Early in 1901, he began to publish the
weekly *Puerto Rico Herald*, in English and Spanish.
Puerto Rico could now speak to her new masters in
their own language, in their biggest city. There was
much to talk about.

The Foraker Act made the island neither a state nor
a territory. Nor did it make the islanders U.S. citizens.
Instead it gave them the specially dreamed-up label
"The People of Puerto Rico." Which meant that the
democratic protections and benefits of the U. S. Constitution did not cover them. They and their island
were entirely under the control of the U. S. Congress,
in which they had no voice and no vote. Compared to
the Spanish Charter of Autonomy, the Foraker Act was
turning out to be a bad deal.

Unemployment and poverty were growing on the island. So were the number of U.S. civil service workers,

paid from Puerto Rico's tax moneys. Big Northern sugar companies were buying up huge parcels of land at prices that were a "steal,"* even though under the Foraker Act no one could own more than five hundred acres. On these plantations men worked a fifteen-hour, forty-five-cent day growing sugar cane.

Muñoz was enraged when Governor Allen said to a Boston newspaper reporter:

"Puerto Rico is a lucky island. It has no public debt and its taxes are enough to cover its budget."

In the *Herald,* Muñoz replied:

Yes, a lucky island on which the people are starving, and from which, not to starve, hundreds of families are emigrating to Cuba, Ecuador, and Hawaii. That Puerto Rico had no public debt is a serious fault. Its good credit standing should be used to put money into circulation and to rebuild its agriculture. As for the taxes with which we balance our budget, Governor Allen does not seem to care how he mows wheat in the field of a stranger, whose ruin is not important.

The Republican leaders were also unhappy with the Foraker law but did not want to back away from their long-standing pro-American policy. They believed they could improve the situation by using their influence as the "in" party. Except for Rosendo Matienzo Cintrón. He urged *Federales* and *Republicanos* to unite. As a single party they would be strong enough to dump the Foraker Act and press for a better deal. Muñoz saw the point and went all out for it in both of his news-

* A hurricane of 1899 bankrupted many Puerto Rican landowners. Muñoz was in Washington when it happened. Without official standing, he negotiated $200,000 in federal aid to hurricane victims.

papers. On February 18, 1904, the Federal Party held a convention, voted itself out of existence, and formed the *Unión de Puerto Rico* (Unionist Party). Matienzo Cintrón and many of his Republican followers joined up at once. In the *Herald,* Muñoz wrote:

> We affirm the right of Puerto Rico to assert its own personality, either through statehood or independence. If the United States continues to humiliate and shame us, we can forget about statehood and support independence, with or without U.S. protection . . . In 1901 only a few of us distrusted the United States. Today all are beginning to realize that we have been deceived. We no longer worship everything that comes from the North.

The chips were down. This was the first party platform to speak of independence. The Republican program remained the same: "Statehood, sooner or later. Let's wait."

The Unionist program had a powerful appeal to Puerto Rico's have-nots in the 1904 election. For the first time, all males over twenty-one could vote, without being able to read and without being taxpayers. There was a Unionist landslide—almost 90,000 against the Republicans' 54,000. In 1906 and 1908, the Unionists won even bigger majorities. Muñoz, back from New York, was elected to the Chamber of Delegates both times.

By 1909 both Unionists and Republicans were insisting that the Foraker Act had to go. To show their unity on this point, Dr. Barbosa and Muñoz embraced each other at a public meeting. It did not last.

In the 1910 elections 59,000 people voted for the Republicans, who still wanted "Americanization." The

Unionists won 100,000 votes. Muñoz Rivera was elected
Resident Commissioner, the island's official spokesman
in Washington. That was the highest office a Puerto
Rican could reach then. Muñoz made it a powerful
position from which to fight for Puerto Rican self-
government.

His first step was to learn English well. As editor
of the Spanish-English *Puerto Rico Herald* in New
York, he had used translators. In those days he was
able to understand a little English, written and spoken,
without help. But as Puerto Rico's chief representative
to the government of the United States, he felt that he
had to master the language. It was a hard year's work
for a man of fifty-one, but he did it. He also studied
the leaders and methods of U.S. federal government.
He made sure he was invited to sit in the congressional
committees whose decisions affected Puerto Rico. (He
had no vote and, usually, no voice.) Privately he talked
to as many congressmen as he could, trying to make
Puerto Rico, its people and their problems real. He
told them, many times, in many ways:

"We will continue to fight against the Foraker Act.
We want Puerto Rico to become a state. Meanwhile,
we want home rule (autonomy). We are patient people,
but if we get neither, we still demand independence."

The congressmen listened, respected him and, privately, shrugged their shoulders until President Woodrow Wilson took office in 1913. His messages to Congress
urged that "justice be done." Then something new was
added—World War I. Though the United States was still
at peace, German submarines were sinking American
ships carrying supplies to England, France, Russia. Ger-

man agents were trying to turn the Latin American countries against the United States. Congress realized that better treatment for Puerto Rico would strengthen the "good neighbor" feeling which the Germans were trying to destroy.

Yet, in January 1916 when Congressman William A. Jones, Virginia Democrat, prepared a new bill to replace the Foraker Act, boos as well as cheers rose among the *Unionistas*. Many thought *El Bill Jones* was too little, too late. Led by the poet, José de Diego, one wing of the party leaned more and more toward independence. In his heart of hearts, that was what Muñoz wanted too. Yet, his five years in Washington told him the chances were zero. The Jones Bill was not Puerto Rico's best bet; it was its only one.

Like all new laws in the making, this one had to go through various committees before it came up for a vote. If the committees improved it and Congress passed it, the bill might prove worthwhile after all. Muñoz worked day and night to make it just that. He attended committee meetings, looked, listened, and argued with the congressmen. At the same time he tried to keep de Diego's pro-independence group from scaring Congress out of its good intentions. Once he was even able to talk to President Wilson. Muñoz's last big effort was a powerful speech to the House of Representatives, in excellent English, on May 5, 1916:

"Give us now the field of experiment which we ask of you . . . it is easy for us to set up a stable republican government with all possible guarantees for all possible interests. And afterwards, when you . . . give us our independence . . . you will stand before humanity as a great creator of new nationalities and a great liberator of oppressed peoples."

The House voted in favor of the Jones Bill. Next, it had to get through the Senate. If it did, the bill would give Puerto Ricans the dignity of U.S. citizenship and a Bill of Rights in line with the U. S. Constitution. Puerto Rico would have its own Legislature—a thirty-nine-man House of Representatives and a nineteen-man Senate. If the governor vetoed a bill passed by the Legislature, the Legislature could go over his head to the President of the United States. The governor would always be Washington's man, but the Puerto Ricans would always have a majority in his cabinet. There were other improvements but the Jones Bill made no promise of future statehood or independence. Just the same, Muñoz felt he was right. It *was* worth the trouble.

His island's business kept him in Washington all through the summer. Sitting at his desk and mopping sweat from his forehead, he longed for the cool hills of his native town. He was tired. In June he wrote to his co-worker, Mariano Abril:

"I read in *La Democracia* that you are returning to Barranquitas. How I envy you! If I could build, not a palace or a mansion but a small house with a bath up here, I would return to my rugged mountains, perhaps forever. I cannot do it. My financial circumstances are tighter today than they were 25 years ago when I first began earning my living as a journalist in Ponce . . . I am continuing to work for the Jones Bill . . ."

And again, in August:

"Your letter with the news from Barranquitas pleased

me very, very much . . . For my final years, of which
there are not many left, I would like to have a patch
of that countryside, under a patch of that sky. As to
politics . . . we will talk about that later, not in San
Juan but up there, in the shade of a tree, in the peace
of a cool evening and in the warmth of a friendship
that will die only when we do, who are still living."

In September there was no longer any doubt that
the Senate, too, would pass the Jones Bill. Muñoz, returning to San Juan, was welcomed at the dock by a
large crowd. He could stay only briefly to acknowledge
the greetings of his countrymen, however.

He had been ill for months, but in Washington he
had not allowed himself to think about it. It might
have interfered with his work. Now he could go home,
to the comfort of "those mountains, that stream, those
starry nights" he had yearned for in his letters. None
too soon. He died in Barranquitas on November 15,
1916. The Jones Bill became law on March 2, 1917.

The people of Puerto Rico knew well the size and
the devotion of Luis Muñoz Rivera's labors. And those
who had been stirred by his poems could read his
Sísifo again and find in it new understanding which
time, without the poet's help, had added. They could
see the difference now between the ancient Sisyphus
and their own. One was a dead spirit doomed to a hell
of hopeless effort. The other was a mortal man whose
lifetime of labor, unfinished, was a triumph. While he
lived, the rock had not crushed him, nor them. Now
it was someone else's turn to brace himself and keep it
moving . . . *up* . . . *up* . . . *up!*

JOSÉ DE DIEGO

CHAPTER 3

The Poet Rebel

The seaport of Aguadilla on the northwest coast of Puerto Rico glories in a legend and a fact. The legend, not always accepted by neighboring towns, is that Christopher Columbus landed there in November 1493. The fact is that José de Diego was born there April 16, 1866. Columbus, discovering the New World, made Puerto Rico a Spanish possession. De Diego, though proud of his Spanish heritage, became the poet and politician of the island's long independence dream.

Three hundred and seventy-three years of Spanish rule passed between these two events. In the first hundred years the island changed a great deal. Under a royal license from Queen Isabella I, the Spaniards began to settle this strangely beautiful green wilderness in the middle of a new unexplored ocean. At first, the Arawak Indians, who lived on the island, were friendly to the men from Spain. Friendship turned to deadly hatred when the newcomers made slave laborers of the Indians to dig gold and cut timber. Hard work, disease, and war against the settlers killed tens of thousands of Indians. Thousands of others, however, intermarried with the Spanish as the years went by. Slaves from Africa were added to the island's population and the work of settling the place went on.

In the next three hundred years life on the island changed very little despite occasional small wars, hurricanes, and cholera epidemics. But just before the beginning of the 1800s, both the Old World and the New were caught up in an age of revolution and change.

One by one, large areas of South America declared their independence from Spain. By 1866 two Caribbean islands, Cuba and Puerto Rico, were all that remained of Spain's vast New World empire. In Cuba, the Ten Years' War for independence was getting ready to happen.* In Puerto Rico, smaller and weaker, a dangerous restlessness was growing. So much so that Spain was willing to listen to the island's grievances. A delegation of Puerto Ricans was invited to come to Madrid. The delegation proposed a program of reforms but warned that no real changes would be possible without the freeing of the slaves. The prime minister listened, sent them home, and did nothing. That was the way things stood the year José de Diego was born.

José's parents were Felipe, a Spanish army officer, and Elisa Martínez, born in Puerto Rico. They died before he was twelve. Until then, his growing-up years were happy ones. Attending the local elementary school didn't make him less happy. He was bright, and the teacher did not expect much. Unlike another schoolboy, the dark-skinned, less prosperous Pepe Barbosa, this Pepe had no need to prove anything to anyone except himself.

In his free time there were places to go that gave a boy's spirit some stretching room. And there were things to see that had more life and beauty in them than he could find on a blackboard. Along the shore he could

* 1868–78. The revolution was finally crushed.

watch fishermen unload their catch . . .

"*Hola,* Paco! Where did you find such an ugly fish?"

"Why ugly?"

"So round and flat. All head and no body."

"True. And a boy who calls his elders by their nick-names runs the risk of becoming all body and no head. To boys, I am Don Francisco."

Pepe could argue with other boys about the rigging of ships that lay at anchor waiting for cargoes of raw sugar, coffee beans, tobacco, fruit . . .

"Look at that barkantine. How she must fly with a stiff wind at her back."

"Sure, she flies. But she's a three-masted bark, not a barkantine. Can't you see her foremast and mainmast are square-rigged?" And the argument would go on until they could find a seaman along the wharf to settle it.

In April, May, and June half of Aguadilla, including Pepe, would go down to the bayside to catch buckets of tiny fish that came by the millions from the Gulf of Mexico to spawn. They were made into fine *pasteles, hayacas,* and other dishes. Any time of year, the treeless hills rising above the ocean's edge a mile from town gave him plenty of sky room for flying kites, his favorite sport.

When he was twelve, José's guardian, Santiago Sanz, sent him off to study at the Polytechnical Institute in Logroño, an old city in northeastern Spain. Just being there was enough to make him feel a foot taller. The hills leading down to the Ebro River were more rugged than the hills at home. The city and the countryside had buildings that were hundreds of years old before

In his free time José would wander down to the wharf and argue with other boys about the rigging of ships that lay at anchor.

Columbus saw Puerto Rico. Next to the school were a convent, a cavalry headquarters, and a bull ring.

For a while, José thought about becoming a bull-fighter. One day he asked a real torero about it. The man looked at him, unsmiling: "Why do you want to be a torero?"

"To face the challenge of life and death, sword in hand, as you do, Don Miguel. It is a noble calling."

"Pah! There are greater callings. A bullfighter grasp-ing a sword can only kill bulls in the ring. But a cou-rageous man, with learning and with a pen in his hand, can topple kingdoms. Go back to your books, *hombre-cito*."

Don Miguel was right. There were such men in Spain. Men such as Emilio Castelar, Francisco Pí y Margall, and José María Orense, who called on the people to get rid of the monarchy and stop living in the past. Queen Isabella II had been forced off the throne. In 1873 Spain became a republic, and the Puerto Rican delegation to the Spanish legislature was finally able to get overwhelming support for a law which abolished "slavery forever in the island of Puerto Rico." As pres-ident, Pí y Margall proposed a very radical program for Spain: separation of church and state; free com-pulsory public schools, abolition of child labor, and laws to protect workers in their dealings with employers.

The republic lasted less than a year. In 1874 the monarchy was back in control, with Alfonso XII as king. But Spain was never the same again. The air remained full of republican words and plans. Going to school in Logroño in the late 1870s, young de Diego looked, listened, read the Spanish newspapers, and found himself caught up in the political excitements of the time and place.

When he was fourteen, he joined the Progressive Republican Committee of Logroño and wrote a humorous article for a pro-republican newspaper. Writing was almost second nature to him. His school notebooks held a growing collection of jingles and poems he composed in classrooms while his teachers were lecturing. At seventeen he got the Bachelor of Arts degree given for credits equaling four years of high school and two years of college work.

"Well, Pepe, what now?" one of his classmates asked. "Back to Puerto Rico to fight Indians?"

"You speak of an earlier time, *amigo*. Today, I am afraid Spaniards fight Spaniards. But no, I am going to Barcelona to study law at the university."

De Diego's life in Barcelona was a merry-go-round of youthful romances, poetry, and politics, with a little time left over, now and then, for his studies. Listening to lectures on Roman law, political economy, or the imperial constitutions of Spain, he continued to write poems in his notebooks. Many of them were about girls. It figured. He was tall, dark, and very good looking. His manners and dress were of a romantic, carefree style that was called "bohemian." There were poems about many girls: Catalina, who would not be moved by his feelings for her; about Lōlilla, a blue-eyed Andalusian singer; about Maruja, a working girl; and Soledad, a gypsy.

Spain was now quieter than it had been in eighty years, but it was still a political volcano. It boiled with arguments among conflicting republican groups, secret anarchist societies, a growing socialist movement, and new trade unions which followed one or another of these political beliefs. De Diego wrote satirical articles and poems against the ruling powers which were made up of the royal family, the nobility, and the church. Among them, these three groups owned most of the land and kept most of the wealth.

De Diego's writings toppled no kingdoms, but they did anger the authorities. Since freedom of the press was something that the government gave or took away, the government flung the young poet into not one but four jails, at Barcelona, Tarragona, Valencia, and Madrid. Released in 1885, he sailed for Puerto Rico to wait until the Spanish police got him off their mind.

He found his home place as pleasant as when he left it. It became more so in December 1886, when he met Carmita Echevarría, "daughter of the blond sun of Aguadilla." He fell very much in love with her but the very respectable Papá Echevarría said, "Never!" He did not consider a radical young bohemian poet to be good son-in-law material. De Diego would not give up, however. To Carmita, he said:

"I am going back to Spain to finish my studies. I will prove to your father that I am worthy of you. Will you stand with me at my mother's grave and promise to wait for me?" Carmita smiled and promised. Returning to Barcelona in 1887, de Diego studied hard and exchanged letters with Carmita for five months. Then he received the unhappy news that she was engaged to marry someone else. In grief and anger he wrote a poem *To Laura* (meaning Carmita). It became one of his

De Diego's writings angered the authorities, and they threw the young poet into jail four different times.

best-known poems. It spoke of "Laura's" promise to wait:

> How lovable you are!
> What an afternoon of that great day!
> What a day of that great afternoon! . . .
> Still I can hear the harmonies
> With which the dance began . . .   [but now]
> Alas, my wounded heart is dying
> As a bird dies, fallen from its nest.

He would love her as long as he lived, the poem said, but he would not come begging for her kindness:

> I know how to struggle, I am young,
> And because I have often crossed the seas,
> I can endure the storm wind's sting upon my face.

But what would happen if she could not help thinking of him and found, too late, that she loved him? Would she ever be happy?

> Bury me very deep, and beware:
> Dead dreams come back to life! . . .
> May you live, may I die. May never the vision
> Of my mourning oppress you in your dreams . . .
> And may God forgive you in heaven
> As I forgive you in Spain.

Sadly, his warning turned out to be more than a poetic expression of grief. Years later he heard that Carmita had never married. She was in a nursing home, mentally ill. Until her death, in 1910, he sent money to provide her with extra comforts.

De Diego's first work in book form was published in 1887. It was *Sor Ana* (Sister Anne), a long poem with a religious theme. But grieving for Carmita and worrying about political events at home made studying impossible for him in Barcelona. He sailed to Cuba and enrolled in the University of Havana.

In Spain, de Diego's political activities had been, to some extent, an intellectual game, a contest of ideas. It gave him the satisfaction of testing his talents in a good cause. In Cuba, his political ideas became clearer, more practical, though no less passionate. The writings of a man named José Martí were passing quietly from hand to hand among the students. Poet, essayist, and revolutionary leader, Martí was considered, even then, to be one of the most remarkable men in the history of all Latin America. Though he dared not set foot on his native Cuban soil for fear of arrest as an enemy of Spain, his name was a living presence on the island.

During fifteen years of exile in New York, Martí wrote countless brilliant articles for the newspapers of South America and for the daily New York *Sun*, as well as poetry of great merit. At the same time he worked, beyond the endurance of a lesser man, to organize a new Cuban freedom movement. Under his leadership, patriotic *Cubanos* put aside their differences, shook off their discouragement, and prepared for a final, successful war of independence.

Events in Cuba raised Puerto Rico's hopes of self-government higher than they had been since 1869, when political parties were formed for the election of the Cortes. For a few years the new Liberal Party had made fairly good progress. After the overthrow of the

Spanish republic of 1873, freedom of politics disappeared. The self-government idea continued to spread quietly, however. The Liberals reorganized in 1887 as the Autonomist Party. Again they were driven underground, this time by the jailings, beatings, and police pressures of *El Año Terrible*.

In 1891, the movement was trying to rebuild itself once more. That was the year de Diego returned, at the age of twenty-five, to practice Spanish law and Puerto Rican patriotism in the city of Mayagüez. Working for Rosendo Matienzo Cintrón, a leading autonomist, it was possible to do both. Still hot with Cuba's independence fever, de Diego joined with Luis Muñoz Rivera and José Celso Barbosa in calling a three-day meeting to decide on a program for Puerto Rico's political future.

There were qualities in this young lawyer that the older men at the conference respected—his education, his talent as a public speaker, his quickness at learning new things. They sensed he would *live* his patriotism by the best rules they would ever lay down for themselves. He did, all his life. In his introduction to *Cantos de Rebeldía* (Songs of Rebellion), a collection of his patriotic poems, he wrote:

I was born in an unfortunate country, a country held in bondage. To the preservation of its life and to the defense of its liberty, I owe my blood which comes from its soil, and my soul which comes from its skies. Though I hold a lyre* I hold it as I would a sword or a hammer or a plow, for I must sing

* A string instrument on which poets accompanied themselves in ancient times.

to my country as though I were brandishing a sword or striking an anvil or cutting a furrow . . .*

The rebellion to which de Diego gave himself was
fierce but nonviolent. It had to be. In Cuba, an island
of 44,000 square miles and three rugged mountain
ranges, a people's guerrilla war against a Spanish army
could be successful. Puerto Rico, thirteen times smaller
(3400 square miles) and having far fewer people, never
stood the same chance. The island had not forgotten
the failure of the three-day uprising at Lares in 1868.
There were many who could still remember the smell
of the dirty prisons at Aguadilla and Arecibo in 1887.

For several years there was little the Autonomists
could do except argue with each other. The hundreds
of debates at conferences and in newspaper articles between 1891 and 1894 could have been summed up
briefly if three leaders had said the following:

Muñoz Rivera: Armed revolution is a nightmare. Win
or lose, it would destroy us. Independence is a beautiful
dream but it just would not work. Let us go on living
with Spain, demanding and getting as much autonomy
as we can. Let's find political allies in Madrid, monarchists or republicans; it does not matter as long as they
will help us in our cause.

Barbosa: I agree with Muñoz Rivera about revolution
and independence. I disagree about much else. Only
Spain's republicans can be trusted to help us in our
struggle toward autonomy. Some monarchists may pre-

---

* Compare the modern folk song: "If I had a hammer, I'd hammer
in the morning/I'd hammer in the evening, all over this land . . ."
(*The Hammer Song*, by Hayes and Seeger. Copyright © 1958 & 1962,
Ludlow Music, Inc., New York. Used by permission.)

tend to be our friends for political reasons of their own. In their hearts they can never want for us what we want for ourselves.

De Diego: Puerto Rico's goal, always, must be independence, which now, sadly, is not within our reach. We must move toward it step by step, year after year. Let the first step be our struggle for autonomy. Watered down, or pure, with the help of monarchists or republicans. It is better to struggle than to hold still. Struggle unites and strengthens us. Let small victories lead us to greater ones.

In 1894 de Diego moved to Arecibo, joined the law office of José Agustín de la Torre, and founded the city's first Autonomist Party organization. He also started a newspaper, *La República* (The Republic), in which he wrote under the name of León Americano (American Lion). His articles and his public speeches did much to reawaken his countrymen's national feeling. For the first time in more than twenty-five years, independence became a word from which Puerto Ricans did not shy away.

Indirectly but definitely de Diego was adding a great deal to the pressure which would make Spain give in to the Autonomists. In 1896 the Cuban revolution was going strong after a year of fighting. Puerto Rican exiles in New York were trying to organize an army of independence of their own. It was widely believed that the fates of both islands were closely tied. The poetess Lola Rodríguez de Tió wrote:

Cuba and Puerto Rico are two wings of the same bird;
Flowers and bullets strike the same heart.

Spain, facing a difficult situation, did some good thinking. This was not 1887. To throw men like de Diego into jail might be like dropping a lighted match into a gasoline tank. The whole island might go BA-RHOOOOM! Maybe it was better to give Puerto Rico its autonomy at once. Otherwise, the independence talk might roll on till peasants with machetes started marching on the town halls trying to take over. On December 4, 1897, a charter of autonomy was officially granted after eighteen months of bargaining between Muñoz Rivera and Prime Minister Sagasta of Spain.

Under the new law Muñoz became the leading secretary in a six-man cabinet, the Executive Council (all Puerto Ricans) formed in February 1898. He appointed José de Diego as Under-Secretary for Justice and Government. In March, there was an election to set up a House of Representatives and a Senate. In April, Spain and the United States were at war. In May, American ships bombarded the city of San Juan. In July, U.S. troops were marching across the island from the south. Civilians were leaving the city, expecting a second bombardment. A Puerto Rican artillery officer named Rivero found Muñoz and de Diego sitting on a bench in the Plaza de Colón the evening of July 30. The three men talked a bit. Rivero said:

"*Adiós, caballeros.* My men and I will be wiped out if McKinley's warships turn their guns on us. They shoot farther and more accurately than our cannons. Since you have permission to live outside of San Juan, I would advise you to leave at once."

Muñoz replied, "As an army officer, you will stay with your cannon to the death. We are officers of civilian government. If death seeks us, it will find us at our posts."

"Naturally," de Diego said, "we remain here."

There was no chance for another attack on the city. Before the American troops reached San Juan, the war ended and Puerto Rico became a U.S. possession.

The Executive Council remained in office until February, 1899. When Muñoz resigned as head of the council because of disagreements with the U.S. military governor, General Henry, the entire cabinet was dismissed. New men were appointed. In May, when Henry was himself replaced by another general, de Diego became district attorney for the Mayagüez region.

Meanwhile, Congress had written a new law, the Foraker Act. This went into effect May 1900. Neither de Diego nor others were very happy about it. It was not a constitution made by and for the people. It was a rule book put together by *norteamericanos* who knew very little about the island. Puerto Ricans felt that, if the Spanish charter of autonomy had been a step toward independence, the Foraker Act was two steps backward.

Nevertheless, de Diego accepted a place in the new cabinet, which now consisted of five Puerto Ricans and six "Northerners." This made the Puerto Ricans a minority in their own government. It also made the Federal Party* of Muñoz and de Diego a minority of the Puerto Rican minority because the six "Northerners" voted with the representatives of Dr. Barbosa's Republican Party. Even worse, the Executive Council could veto any law passed by the new Chamber of Dele-

* From 1897 to 1899 it was called the Liberal Party.

gates.* This meant that the six U.S. men, who could always outvote the five Puerto Ricans in the Executive Council, held the real power to run Puerto Rico.

De Diego attended a few sessions to see how it would work out. In his opinion, it did not. He resigned. But beginning in 1902 he was elected from Mayagüez to the Chamber of Delegates continuously until 1918. And from 1909 to 1918, he was the Chamber's presiding officer or speaker.

In 1901 he married Georgina Blanes. He was thirty-five then, one of the island's three most influential leaders, and an able specialist in criminal law.

Puerto Ricans still chuckle about the crushing rebuke de Diego, for the defense, gave to a prosecuting attorney from the States. Addressing the jury, the "Northerner" repeatedly referred to the prisoner as "this Negro." De Diego, in his turn, persisted in speaking of "this red-haired Kentuckian" until the prosecutor protested to the judge:

"What does the color of my hair or my place of birth have to do with this matter?"

"Exactly the same thing as the color of my client's skin," de Diego retorted. "My learned colleague must understand that here in Puerto Rico juries do not deliberate on the color of a man's skin. They deliberate on the evidence!" And it was on the evidence that de Diego's client was acquitted.

The longer the Foraker Act lasted the less Puerto Ricans liked it. It was making their lives a little better

* Similar to state legislatures in the United States.

in a few ways but much worse in many others. Both
the Unionist Party* led by Muñoz and de Diego, and
the Republican Party of Dr. Barbosa agreed on this.
But what to do instead? On this question the two
groups disagreed bitterly, as always.

"The real answer," said the Republicans, "is for Puerto
Rico to join the United States *as a state*. We will be
more prosperous, healthier and better educated if we
integrate our island with the United States."

The Unionist Party program had more "stretch" to
it. It said, in effect: "Congress is not about to make
Puerto Rico a state. Our first move must be for *complete*
self-government under U.S. protection. Anyway we
would want solid proofs that our people could have
full equality in American life. If, in the future, the
United States goes on refusing us the democracy of
which it is so proud, we are prepared to raise the
banner of independence."

De Diego did not wait for some far-off time. Within
the Unionist Party and throughout the island, he kept
the issue alive. To this lawyer, politician, and poet, independence was more than a political idea. He was an
educated man who read Latin and French as easily as
Spanish. His private library held nine thousand books.
He had the deep feeling that only a scholar could have
for the Spanish-speaking culture in which he had been
brought up. He would never say yes to any kind of
political autonomy which did not also guarantee Puerto
Rico's cultural independence. But, what did one have
to do with the other?

* The Federal Party became the Unionist Party in 1904.

What *is* culture when you get right down to it? A culture is the style of living and thinking that a people slowly, over a period of hundreds of years, makes and remakes for itself by the way it earns its living and by the ways in which it uses its language, literature, music, art, and religion. It comes from the everyday wisdom of farmers and workers, from the ideas, writings, and actions of its best thinkers; from the work of its scientists, from the worthiness or worthlessness of its rulers. And all the time, while a people is making and remaking its culture, the culture is making and remaking them. It is a process, connected to a thousand years of yesterdays. And it goes on endlessly, today, tomorrow. This is what makes a place and a people belong to each other. It is their culture that gives meaning to a people's words when they say "we are we," or to a man's, when he says "I am I. Tomorrow I will be more than I am today!" If de Diego could help it, he would never permit anyone to separate Puerto Ricans from their Spanish-American heritage and tie them, instead, to what he felt was the barbaric culture of *El Norte*.

Year after year he went on singing to his country as though he were "brandishing a sword or striking an anvil." Looking at his island under United States rule, he saw more schools, more roads, and a few more public health clinics. He also saw more and more land passing into the ownership of large American companies, even though the Foraker Act made it illegal for any corporation to control more than five hundred acres.

Mostly he saw the same old illiteracy, sickness, poverty; the same dreary life in which people were born

old and died young. This he saw especially among the
large class of *jíbaros,* the easily ruled peasant folk who
lived on *café puya* (coffee, black and bitter) and a slice
of bread for breakfast, a piece of sugar cane or a tomato
in the fields at midday, with rice and beans for supper.
The green hills and the rolling fields of his island must
not be a nesting place for such misery. Those who have
the strength to endure such a life must also have the
anger and the courage to change it, de Diego thought.
This was the message of his poem, *En la Brecha* (In
the Breach), which he addressed "To a Victim of Oppression." Those who read it understood that he was
speaking not just to one *jíbaro* or a thousand but also
to the island itself—to the place called, lovingly, Borinquen.

Alas, unfortunate! If suffering dismays you,
If leaden weariness weighs down your limbs,
Learn from the winter-withered tree: grow green again!
And like the buried seed, reclaim your right to live!

Yes, live again! Breathe, shout, walk, fight,
Vibrate, glide, thunder; outshine the noonday sun.
Do what the rain-rich river does: become a flood!
Or like the sea on rocky shores: strike tirelessly!

Know how to face the angry thrust of hurricanes,
Not bawling like the lamb, unshepherded, in sorrow,
But roaring your defiance as the wild beast roars.

Rise up! Revolt! Resist!
Speak with the awesome voice of the tormented bull!
Or keeping deadly silence—Charge!

In another poem, *Aleluyas* (Halleluiahs), he expressed his bitter resentment against the superior attitude of the United States toward the people and the culture of Puerto Rico. Addressing himself "To the Gentlemen from the North," he wrote:

Gentlemen from the marvelous and fruitful North;
The Caribbean islands are also part of America.
These islands, too, were here from the Beginning, when
God raised them from the sea and made them beautiful.
After centuries, coming somewhere from the East,
the Indians found the islands and the continent.
And after other centuries, the ships of Spain arrived . . .

Facing the Puritan ships which followed after,
the Spanish boats were pigmy-sized,
especially on that day when the Spanish people
sank, ships and all, in the seas of America;
that day when you came in all your splendor,*
you, the very powerful Gentlemen from the North.

Forgive the heavens and earth, Gentlemen,
for having formed these islands so long before the war . . .
Forgive that so many of us had already been born
without assistance from the U.S.A.—
born in America, with nothing to rely upon
except the kindness God was bold enough to show us.

We are not the strongest, nor are we the masters,
but we are the sons of Conquistadors . . .
We know about the mysteries of philosophy
and about the Art that governs holy Poetry . . .

* De Diego is referring to the defeat of Spain by the U.S. in the Spanish-American War (1898).

But we know nothing in this, the Country of the Sun,
about the art of government as practiced in Tammany Hall.
Nor do we know the topsy-turvy thinking by which
you stretch the California boundary to the Philippines . . .

Watching you put history through such flip-flops
leaves us ignorant of the language and the meaning
of the English peoples. We speak another language,
with other thoughts. And we have been telling you,
for a long time, to please go to the devil,
and leave us with God!

In addition to *Sor Ana,* of his student days, three collections of de Diego's poems were published in his lifetime: *Pomarrosas* (Rose Apples) in 1904 and *Jovillos** in 1916. His *Cantos de Rebeldía* (Songs of Rebellion) also appeared that year. It opens with *The Last String,* a poem in which he pledges to go on using his poet's lyre as a patriotic weapon. With the passing of the years and the setbacks of political struggle, the strings of his lyre break, one after another, until only one is left, but:

That string is in my hand.
I touch it and I treat it carefully.
It will remain in my hoarse lyre till death,
The highest gift that fate can give a bondsman . . .
A long, strong string!
A string that's long and strong,
For the tyrant's neck!

A fifth collection, *Cantos de Pitirre* (Songs of the King-

* *Jovillos* comes from the word *jobo* or "Jew plum," a fruit which grows along every country roadside. Among Puerto Rican schoolboys, "eating *jobos*" is the phrase for "cutting classes."

bird), was not published until 1950.

More and more de Diego's feeling for independence became a passion for Puerto Rico's right to its own deep-down Spanish way of living and thinking—its own culture. In 1916 he founded the Antillean* Academy of the Language, to preserve the purity of written and spoken Spanish. He did not object to the study of English as a "foreign language" in the Puerto Rican schools. He fought bitterly, however, against making English the classroom tongue in which all other subjects were taught.

That same year, though he was not well, de Diego participated in the three hundredth anniversary celebration of the work of Miguel de Cervantes, Spain's most famous writer. For his addresses to learned gatherings in Barcelona and Madrid, the Puerto Rican poet was given the honorary title of *Caballero de la Raza* (Nobleman of the Spanish People). Returning to his home, he sought medical advice about his still-failing health. Examination showed that he had filariasis, a deadly disease carried by mosquitoes in the tropics. He began a slow, losing fight for life. Finally he went to New York City for additional treatment. The beginning of July 1918 found him there, bedridden, with no hope of recovery.

For him, the end was close at hand. For Puerto Rico, independence was as far off as ever. But de Diego refused to believe that his people did not really care about independence. He died on July 16, 1918, neither afraid

* The Antilles, which include Puerto Rico, are the chain of islands which form the northern boundary of the Caribbean Sea.

nor defeated, but murmuring phrases from his sonnet, *Ultima Acto* (The Final Deed).

When death commands, let Borinquen's green shield
be proudly lowered to my grave with me.
My shroud? The bright-hued flag that cried "Be Free"
to men who stood on freedom's battlefield.
Above my burial place, where songbirds wheeled,
a lonely hope, as patient as the sea,
shall test the patience of eternity;
yet, on a day, my tomb shall be unsealed.
Then will I hear again hope's full-voiced cry.
Then will I harvest from my bleached remains
the shield; then raise my noble shroud on high,
a talisman against my country's chains,
to say, unchallenged, to infinity;
This earth, this sea, this sky, is Borinquen's.

De Diego returned home to Puerto Rico, where a doctor told him he was dying.

LUIS MUÑOZ MARÍN

CHAPTER 4

A Man of the People

Through the spaces in the balcony railing, the little boy looked down at the crowd in the street. The crowd looked up, not at him but at his father, who sat sipping coffee. Every few minutes a man would push to the front and call out the results of the voting in one district or another:

"*Partido Unión de Puerto Rico—2731; Partido Republicano—1589.*"

His father would smile and wave his thanks. As the hour grew later, the messengers followed each other more quickly. The crowd grew larger, more excited. "*Viva la Unión! Viva Muñoz!* Speak to us, Don Luis!" The love and respect he heard in those cries thrilled the tired six-year-old to wide-awakeness. And his father's voice had never rung so richly as it did now:

"My friends, it seems certain that we have won a majority. But we must understand that this election victory of November 1904 is a first step, not a final one."

The boy felt Doña Amalia's hand, lightly, on his shoulder. "Bedtime, Luisito. Come." He followed her to his room asking, "Mamá, will *stay* in San Juan, now?"

"No questions, *niño*. For you this is the end of the evening." She could not guess at the excitement swirling in his large round head. She could not know how deeply he had looked into the upturned faces of the crowd.

Otherwise she might have said, "This evening is the beginning of my son's future."

Luis Muñoz Marín was born February 18, 1898, in San Juan. Political discussions were his nursery rhymes and his lullabies. Luis was three when his parents moved to New York City and his father started the *Puerto Rico Herald*. He was hardly five when his father's friends, for the fun of it, taught him to shout, "*Muera Barbosa!*" (Down with Barbosa!). Papá Muñoz was upset because, politics aside, he and the Republican leader were friends. He scolded the boy and taught him, instead, to say, "*Viva Barbosa.*"

During his years in New York, little Luis learned to speak a fair amount of English, with a Manhattan accent. He was eight when the family returned to San Juan. During the next four years he attended the private school run by Don Pedro Moczó.

"Luis always behaved like a poet," one of his schoolmates remembered. "At lunch, he would stop eating and stare into space. Sometimes he would get so absentminded that he would scratch his head with his fork."

At least once, the schoolmaster sent a note to Papá Muñoz: "Your son is very bright but he is undisciplined." In 1910, Don Pedro's worries about the boy came to an end. Muñoz Rivera, elected Puerto Rico's Resident Commissioner in the United States, took his wife and son to live in the nation's capital.

Washington was spacious, calm, beautiful. It had strength and dignity. Just walking through the streets was an adventure. Almost any building worth looking at stood for something more than itself and there were hundreds of them. For instance, there was this huge building on Pennsylvania Avenue and Seventeenth Street —a long block long, and a short block wide. It had so many columns, porches, chimneys, and so much fancy stonework that it made him dizzy to look up at it. Out front, on the Seventeenth Street side, were four cannon captured from the Spanish troops in Cuba in 1898. Inside was the War Department. From somewhere inside that building came the order that sent General Nelson A. Miles and sixteen thousand U.S. troops to Puerto Rico when Luis was barely six months old. Some of them were still there, at Fort Brooke, in San Juan.

There were other important-looking buildings on Pennsylvania Avenue. He pictured Yankee officials sitting at large desks, deciding what should be done and what should not be done in Puerto Rico. But how could they know what to decide? Washington and Puerto Rico were so different, so far from each other. Not even the language was the same.

On his way home from such explorations his questions would multiply until he was heavy-headed. Why did the United States take his island away from Spain in the first place? If there were Yankee soldiers in Puerto Rico, why were there no Puerto Rican soldiers? Why didn't the Yankees say his father's name right—Seh-*nyor Mooh*-nyos—instead of See-nor *Mew*-nose or, worse, Mr. Rye-*vee*-ra? Would Puerto Rico ever get the self-government that his father kept writing about in *La Democracia?*

He already knew some of the answers. But every answer that took hold in his mind sprouted new questions. Coming home late in the evening, the resident commissioner would stop in the living room, where his son's bed was made up on a couch. There would be long talks between them about government and politics, about Puerto Rico's past, and about its future. It could have been these first years of lifelong questioning and answer-seeking that once made Luis Muñoz Marín say, with a wink:

"General Miles and I came to Puerto Rico in the same year, but I learned more."

His father's two-time re-election as resident commissioner kept the family in Washington almost six years. Luis attended Georgetown College for three years, from 1911 to 1914, but his father's death, in 1916, put an end to thoughts of any further schooling. Puerto Rico's grief matched his own. The meaning of his father's life had become quite clear to him. As though wishing to console the hundreds of thousands who mourned with him, he wrote:

> I would be a giant, to embrace the mountains that he contemplated in his boyhood, the mountains that shelter his countrymen . . . a giant to complete the work of Luis Muñoz Rivera.

The father died richer in his country's love than in the world's goods. He left his wife and son four hundred dollars in ready money. Doña Amalia settled in San Juan, living on a small income from *La Democracia*. Luis returned to Washington, as secretary to the new resident commissioner.

During his Georgetown days the youth had quietly cultivated his talent as a writer both in Spanish and English. While he was still nineteen, two books of his

Spanish writings were published, *Borrones* (Sketches) and *Madre Haraposa* (Mother in Rags). Now writing was no longer just something he *wanted* to do; it was something he *had* to do. The more he wrote, the more he wanted to live in New York. The city was a magnet that pulled mightily at the minds of young writers and artists, and Greenwich Village was the core of the magnet. In 1918, that is where he went.

The life of a free-lance poet and journalist barely out of his teens had its ups and downs—mostly downs. But living off of 30 cents' worth of hamburger and onions on days when money was tight had its good points, too.

"When I knew I could do that, I knew I was a free man," Muñoz recalled many years later. He was free, for instance, to be the editor of *La Revista de Indias* (Review of the Indies), a magazine of Latin-American prose, poetry, and opinion. That is where the hamburger money came from. And that was where he met Muna Lee, a talented young American poet who did translations for him. They were married on July 1, 1919.

During most of the 1920s, whenever they were living in New York, their home was a gathering place for a widening, changing circle of remarkable and talented people. Some were still young and unknown, others were already famous.

They enjoyed long evenings of lively discussion about life—art, science, politics, religion, economics. Often the talk turned to Latin-America and especially to Puerto Rico. At such moments, young Muñoz spoke quietly, brilliantly. Yet, despite the sympathy on the faces of his listeners, he would feel inwardly restless, dissatisfied.

These were people who understood the world and the way mankind lives in it. But could he make them *really* understand how much and how desperately Puerto Rico needed to be changed? He did his best to explain. . . .

As a U.S. possession, Puerto Rico was producing more and enjoying it less—seven times as much sugar cane, much more molasses, rum, citrus fruits, needlework. The value of the goods Puerto Rico sold to the United States increased every year—from less than $20,000,000 worth in 1899 to almost $112,000,000 worth in 1921.

So what was wrong?

Much of the best farm land and most of the crops belonged to four U.S. sugar companies and one U.S. tobacco company. They did not bring the profits from the sales of these crops back to Puerto Rico. They preferred to invest their profits in other parts of the world. The island became more and more a huge sugar cane farm. Other crops were crowded out. Food became more expensive because it had to be shipped from the States. The island's population kept increasing, but the jobs did not multiply as fast as the people. This kept wages very low. Men in the cane fields were paid as little as eleven cents an hour. Even as close to the present as 1940, they seldom earned more than $230 a year. Life on the island was hard, yet there seemed to be no way out.

Muñoz, being a poet and a journalist, could not help writing about Puerto Rico any more than he could help breathing. During the 1920s his articles about his island's problems appeared in the Sunday editions of the Baltimore *Sun, The Smart Set, The Nation,* the *New Republic,* and *The American Mercury.* Full of facts, figures, and arguments, his articles tried to make U.S. readers understand what his native island needed. And he wrote poems, hoping to make them feel a little of what he felt. One of them was called *Pamphlet*.

I have broken the rainbow
against my heart
as one breaks a useless sword against a knee . . .
I have drowned my dreams
. . . to glut the dreams that sleep for me in the veins
of men who have sweated and wept and raged
to season my coffee . . .
The dream that sleeps in breasts stifled by tuberculosis
    (A little air, a little sunshine!)
the dream that dreams in stomachs cramped by hunger
    (A bit of bread, a bit of white bread!)
the dream of bare feet
    (Fewer stones on the road, Lord, fewer
    broken bottles!)
the dream of calloused hands
    (Moss . . . clean cambric . . . things smooth, soft,
    soothing!)
The dream of trampled hearts
    (Love . . . Life . . . Life!)

I am the pamphleteer of God,
God's agitator,
And I go with the mob of stars and hungry men
toward the great dawn . . .

Muñoz knew that printed words were not enough. Puerto Rico needed political leadership and action. But what kind? The Republican and Unionist parties did nothing but argue about statehood and independence. They ran in elections and made promises to the voters.

They were careful, however, not to get on the wrong side of the big landowners who gave money to their campaign funds.

On a visit to Puerto Rico, Muñoz met Santiago Iglesias Pantín, leader of the Socialist Party. He went with Iglesias to speak at a meeting of cane workers who had gone on strike demanding a few more cents an hour. Facing this audience in an open field under a warm sun was very different than talking to a circle of his highly educated friends in his New York apartment. His New York friends listened with open minds. These strikers, his countrymen, were listening with empty bellies. As he spoke, he could see a challenge in their eyes:

"Okay, Don Luis. What can you tell us about our troubles that we do not know better than you? How can you *help* us?"

"As a journalist," he said, "I pledge myself to tell the people of the North, in their language, about your struggle." When they applauded, he felt relieved, as though he had passed a test.

Returning to New York, he thought, "Iglesias might have the answer," but he was in for a disappointment. The Socialists were busy forming a political partnership with the Republicans against the Unionists. By 1924, Muñoz found it hard to tell one party from another. In 1926 he was back in San Juan as editor of *La Democracia*. He wrote straight-out articles about low wages, unemployment, bad living conditions, and do-nothing government officials until he made the leaders of all three political parties uneasy. He was rocking the boat so hard that they had to find a way to stop him.

Muñoz went into the fields and promised the sugar cane workers help in their fight for higher wages and better working conditions.

In August 1927, Muñoz was sent on a special mission to the States to interest investors in starting new industries on the island. Nothing came of it. That year and the next two were "boom" years when U.S. big businessmen were making their highest profits ever. They did not want more factories, just more customers, to keep the good times going.

Muñoz, his wife, and their two children remained in the States for several years. He wrote magazine articles and worked as an editor for the Associated Press. Meanwhile he studied, often admiringly, this rich, clever giant of a nation which always seemed so sure of itself. But late in 1930, touring around in a beat-up automobile, he saw fear and bewilderment on the face of America. Factories and banks were closing. Farms lay idle. City governments had no money to pay their teachers, firemen, trash collectors. Millions were unemployed. America was plunging straight down into the Great Depression of the Thirties, and it looked like nothing was ever going to break the fall.

In Puerto Rico it was far worse. Everything had just about hit bottom—jobs, wages, living conditions, the spirits of the political parties and their ability to do anything about anything. More than half of the people (three out of five) were out of work. Muñoz saw only one real hope for the future:

"I want my people to want independence. Once they do want it they will begin to struggle for the improvement of their own lives."

Returning to the island in August 1931, he joined a new Liberal Party being formed by ex-*Unionistas* who favored independence. He was just the man they needed to strengthen their ticket. The elections of November 1932 sent Luis Muñoz Marín to the Puerto Rican Senate and put Franklin D. Roosevelt in the White House.

The four years that followed were a time of new and desperate government problems in the United States— how to protect small farmers from losing their farms; how to find jobs for the jobless; how to decide fair prices for goods and fair wages for work, so that sellers could afford to sell and workers could afford to buy. Meanwhile the federal government had to form relief agencies to put some beans and bread on the table and a roof overhead for millions who could not make it any other way. This was the New Deal and the Roosevelt administration was willing to cut Puerto Rico in. But Robert H. Gore, the new governor, just was not interested.

Muñoz, thirty-four, and Antonio Barceló, the veteran politician, started a "Governor Gore, go home!" campaign in *La Democracia*. Then Muñoz carried the protest directly to President Roosevelt. Gore was forced to resign, but the young liberal remained in Washington for a while, meeting U.S. cabinet members and top New Deal officials. Before leaving, he wrote to Mrs. Roosevelt, who was very much interested in Puerto Rican affairs:

"There is in Puerto Rico a generation that is coming to power in all political parties . . . It wants to fight hunger, not with doles but with social justice . . . It wants to break the stranglehold of land monopoly and restore the soil to the people who work it. It wants to diversify crops, plant food . . . emancipate the people from sugar. It wants industrial development to give dignity and purpose to political action."

The ideas in Muñoz's letter soon took more definite form under a special commission headed by Dr. Carlos Chardón. The big sugar growers refused to help it. So did the coalition* of Republicans and Socialists to whom the growers quietly paid their dues in big folding-money. Washington did help the Chardón Plan get started, but Muñoz spent much of the next four years trying to keep it from being beaten to death. The only real work it managed to get done was to supply food to thousands of the island's worst-off families.

In those desperate Depression years, the failure of the Chardón Plan gave the small tough Nationalist Party of Albizu Campos a chance to win popularity. The Nationalists said, "Independence now, with no strings or favors. We have nothing to lose." For this they were willing to go into the streets with guns in their hands. But steps were taken in the U. S. Senate to cool the independence issue. Millard Tydings, of Maryland, introduced a bill for a special election in which Puerto Ricans would vote for or against *immediate* independence. If independence won, all U.S. help would stop at once. A 25 per cent import tax would be slapped on all Puerto Rican sugar shipped to the United States. This would shut the island out of its biggest market for its most important product. Tens of thousands of Puerto Ricans would face starvation.

The Nationalists said, "Fine. Since the U.S. admits our independence, what's to vote on? Let's start organizing our new government."

* A partnership between two or more parties working together to keep control of a government.

The Senate finally defeated the Tydings bill. But in the months before that, the bill caused sharp political conflicts on the island. Barceló, head of the Liberal Party, said bitterly, "If that is all we can expect from the United States, let us take it, even if we starve." Muñoz said, "No! this is not an honest offer. I do not want independence under the threat of starvation. I want independence with economic guarantees that will allow Puerto Ricans to survive with dignity." The differences between the two men could not be solved, and the Liberal Party was destroyed as a result. Muñoz and those few who agreed with him found themselves alone, without a party and without an organization.

What would happen now to Muñoz's dream of a new deal for Puerto Rico? Where would he find the power to make it real? Unlike other politicians Muñoz believed that the largest class of Puerto Ricans—the hundreds of thousands of poor farmers and field laborers, the *jíbaros,* and their city cousins were their own best hope. Getting together and sticking together, they could build a new kind of political party. And *that* was where the power would be. But somebody had to get it started. He would become, in real life, the pamphleteer, the agitator. He would "go with the mob of stars and hungry men toward the great dawn . . ." As great as they could make it, anyway. With him went the handful of talented young ex-Liberals, many of whom have since become famous in their own right.

Muñoz the politician began to turn the "mob" of Muñoz the poet into an organization such as Puerto Rico had never seen before—*El Partido Popular Dem-*

ocrático (The Popular Democratic Party)—the *Populares*, for short. Their emblem was a man wearing a *pava*, the big home-woven straw hat of farm workers in the fields. Three words went with the picture: *PAN —TIERRA—LIBERTAD* (Bread—Land—Liberty). By July 1938 they were ready to put candidates on the ballot in two election districts. That left them only 784 districts to go before the 1940 elections.

Was there any chance at all? *La Democracia,* Muñoz's paper, was out of business. The *Populares* had no money to print their message, mail it, or broadcast it on the radio. They would have to hit the road and *preach* it, on every hill, in every hollow across the island. They did just that, the hard way, finding food and beds where they could, collecting pennies for gas and oil from their audiences. It was tough going all the way, and their battle cry soon became *jalda arriba!* (up the hill!). Muñoz himself spoke countless times, in five hundred election districts. These were meetings at which the listeners also talked and the speakers also listened—and learned.

"Don Luis," said a *jíbaro* at one meeting, "why is it that the men we elect never do anything to help us? Is it, perhaps, because so many of us have always sold our votes to them?"

"Yes, that is why! Where does the man who buys so many votes get the money? He gets it from those who refuse to give you justice. When he is elected, he must serve *them*, not you. Two dollars and justice cannot come to you from the same hand!"

"And if we do not sell our votes, Don Luis?"

"Then you can *lend* them to me, and I shall be in debt to *you.*"

Muñoz knew it was not stupid greed that made the *jíbaros* sell their votes. It was hunger. He would have to prove to them, over and over, that their power to think together and vote together was worth far more than a few pounds of rice and beans.

"Never trust a politician," he would say. "Not even me. But since you like the program of the *Populares*, elect us—and watch us. If you feel no difference in your lives in the next four years, throw us out." His listeners would murmur their surprise and approval. But when he spoke of independence, they would stare at him silently, and he at them. In their famished faces he could read the reason for their silence. To them the issue was bread, not independence. He quickly learned to concentrate on the bread-and-butter issues.

Muñoz and his men wrote out twenty-two new laws. Before a crowd of fifteen thousand in San Juan, every *Popular* candidate solemnly swore to fight for the passage of these laws if he were elected. The party also handed out thousands of copies of its program, saying to the voters: "Keep this and use it as a score card to check our actions against our promises." By late 1940, the *Populares* had grown from a little splinter group to a major political force. Muñoz was big news and the island's radio network had to invite him to speak. On November 3, he told listeners:

"Weeks, months, years, I have been at this work so that you might learn . . . The only way to end the misery, the insecurity, the injustice you have suffered lies in your hands. This part of my work is finished.

Now it is up to you! Have faith in yourselves! Believe in yourselves!"

The *Populares* won a remarkable though incomplete victory. Muñoz became president of the Senate in which his party now had ten out of nineteen seats. They won only eighteen out of thirty-nine seats in the House of Representatives, two less than a majority. It was enough for a start. But hard times and big problems did not disappear overnight. In fact, new problems arose as the United States entered World War II in December 1941. Supplies of food and other goods ran short because there were not enough American ships and too many German submarines in the waters separating Puerto Rico from the United States. Just the same, things began to happen.

The sales tax and the tax on salt were removed. Land and houses worth less than a thousand dollars also became tax-free. A new income tax law was passed which collected more from those who could afford it and less from those who could not. New government agencies were set up to manage Puerto Rico's affairs in new ways: a Minimum Wage Commission, a Planning Board, an Industrial Development Corporation, a Government Development Bank, and Land, Water Resources, Communications, and Transportation Authorities.

In the 1944 elections Muñoz and his party won seventeen out of nineteen Senate seats and thirty-seven out of the thirty-nine seats in the House of Representatives.

The old law limiting private landowners to five hundred acres each began to be enforced at last. Under a new law, the Land Authority took over 110,000 acres of sugar land and two mills. The wages it paid to thousands of field workers, and the low prices it charged small farmers for grinding their cane set an example which the big private planters had to follow.

The government settled some 18,000 landless families, 90,000 persons altogether, into 143 new villages where they now had small plots of land on which to grow food for themselves or for sale. And there were 89 new medical centers; an additional 1500 hospital beds; 3000 more schoolteachers and 2000 more schoolrooms; free school lunches for nearly 200,000 children. New city housing projects were being built for 30,000 people living in leaky shacks. There was electricity in 150 country districts which had lived by candlelight and muscle power. A *jíbaro* who saw the lines running from a new generating plant through his native hills said, "These wires bring light into our hearts." Such were the beginnings of the program now known as "Operation Bootstrap."

In those early years Muñoz and the *Populares* had a powerful ally, Rexford Guy Tugwell, who, from 1941 to 1946 was the best U.S. governor the island ever had. He backed Muñoz all the way.

In 1947, the strength of what was happening moved Congress to pass a new law:

"At the general election in 1948 and at each such election . . . thereafter the Governor of Puerto Rico shall be elected by the qualified voters of Puerto Rico . . ."

Muñoz was the first, by a huge majority. Who else? The *jíbaros* and the *obreros* (workers) loved him because he respected them. They could tell true stories such as this about him: He was resting in a friend's country house, exhausted by the campaign, when a *jíbaro* came to him. "Don Luis," the man said, "I vowed that if you were elected I would kneel to the Virgin Mary in your presence. *Con permiso."*

Muñoz replied. "Then we will both kneel." When they rose and the man left the room one of Don Luis's aides whispered to him, "That fellow sold his last two chickens to get here. He will have many miles to walk unless we give him bus fare." Don Luis shook his head: "No. When a man offers you his soul you do not hand him change. Take my car and drive him home."

During these years of struggle, an important change took place in his personal life, too. An estrangement had grown up between him and the talented Muna Lee, who returned to Washington to follow a career of her own. At the time of his election he was already married to Inés Mendoza, a schoolteacher, a fiery independence supporter and an early *Populares* member.

In Africa and Asia many colonies held by the big nations were becoming independent. Neither the U. S. Government nor the Puerto Ricans could allow the rest of the world to go on thinking of Puerto Rico as a colony. So, the old debate—statehood or independence—grew hot again. But Muñoz was convinced by now that sudden independence would mean sudden death to the island's future prosperity. It could not rebuild its life without help from the United States. At the same time, he strongly believed that his people needed the fullest possible self-government to succeed in their self-improvement program.

Muñoz, elected the first governor of Puerto Rico, knelt with a jíbaro in thanks before the Virgin Mary.

"Let's work out a new arrangement about this question of where we and the U.S. stand with each other," said Muñoz and the *Populares.* "Then we can get on with the main job of producing more and better food, clothing, houses, water supply, electricity, health care, education, social benefits."

The new arrangement began with the passing of Public Law 600 by Congress in 1950. It was a "compact," or agreement, with the people of Puerto Rico. They would go on being U.S. citizens. The U.S. would recognize their right to draw up a new constitution and to organize a new government. The island's voters accepted this offer. A convention of specially elected delegates from all over the island met to write a new constitution. The first section of Article I said:

"The Commonwealth of Puerto Rico is hereby constituted. Its political power emanates from the people . . ." The word Commonwealth had a special meaning in this document—Puerto Rico was keeping its close ties with the United States of its own free will. On July 25, 1952, exactly fifty-four years after U.S. troops landed at Guánica, Governor Muñoz proclaimed the commonwealth to be officially in existence.

Meanwhile, he and his economic advisers, Teodoro Moscoso and Rafael Picó, were struggling with the problem of starting new industries. Using government funds had not worked very well. The money to build and run hundreds of new factories would have to come from private investors in the States. To find such investors and to develop new profitable industries would take more time. The voters gave Muñoz and his *Populares* the time that was needed by re-electing them in

1952, 1956, and 1960. By the end of his fourth term, Puerto Rico had more than 1000 new factories, providing more than 70,000 new jobs. Per capita* income had jumped from $122 a year to $830 in 1965. It was becoming usual for people to live to the age of seventy instead of forty-six, which had been the ordinary length of Puerto Rican lifetimes until 1940. In ten years the government had built new housing for 135,000 people, and more was being built every day. Education had also become a big industry, one for which the island spent $120,000,000 during Muñoz's last year as governor.

In August 1964, most Puerto Ricans needed no college education to know that their island was not exactly heaven. There were still large numbers of unemployed. One-third of the population still lived in run-down, crowded, and often unsanitary housing. The quality of education needed to be improved. But they knew something else, too. Their island was far better off than it had ever been. Wherever they turned, they could see the signs. Some nine thousand *Populares* met in the Isidoro García ball park that month to nominate candidates for the next election. They expected Don Luis to lead the ticket again. As he rose to speak everyone held up four fingers and chanted, *"Cuatro más! Cuatro más!"*—"Four more!" (years). Only gradually, as he spoke, did they realize that he was refusing to run.

"It is time to go back to the classroom, to the Senate; to the road along the mountain, along the clearing, to get close to the people again."

A roar of astonishment and grief exploded in the ball

* The amount each man, woman, and child would have if the island's total income for the year were evenly divided.

park. "No! No! *Cuatro más! Cuatro más!*" And the old battle cry *"Jalda arriba!"* Doña Inés pleaded with the crowd to hear her husband out. Then the governor explained his thinking. To keep one man in office too long puts democracy in danger. They must not depend on his personal leadership but on themselves and their party. The delegates finally understood. They gave the nomination to Roberto Sánchez Vilella, a fifty-one-year-old, States-educated civil engineer who had spent most of his career as Muñoz's chief aide. Sánchez and the *Populares* won by their usual huge majority that November and Muñoz went back to the Senate.

Approaching the age of seventy, he remained a senator and the leader of his party. His place in the common history of Puerto Rico and the United States was already secure. It is the special place of a man who helps his people discover their own power, gives them hope and leads them up the hill.

To look back and see how far and how bravely they had climbed together—that was satisfaction enough for any man's lifetime, even a great man's. But there was something more. He could look ahead and see them climbing other hills, the hills of the future. He could feel confident that they would know how.

Index